PARR
and the seamy side of magic

KC Ellis, in a reversal of literary norms, writes under his own name and lives the rest of his life under a pseudonym. His formative years were spent under the influence of *Monty Python*, *Not The Nine O'Clock News*, *The Young Ones* and *The Hitch Hiker's Guide to the Galaxy,* sharpening his wit among his siblings, most of whom are still willing to speak to him.

As one fourth of a formation luggage team he made Terry Pratchett laugh, and won a prize for it. Terry Pratchett's novels often make him laugh but, unfairly, Terry has never been given a prize for that.

PARRY HOTTER
and the seamy side of magic

K C Ellis

www.parryhotter.com

A Novel

Phantom Genius Ltd

www.phantomgenius.com

First published 2002 by Phantom Genius Ltd
The White House
Clifton Marine Parade
Gravesend, Kent DA11 0DY

www.phantomgenius.com

Copyright © Phantom Genius Ltd 2002
All rights reserved.

First Edition

The right of K C Ellis to be identified as the author of this work has been asserted by him in accordance with the Copyright, Designs and Patents Act 1988.

This book is a work of fiction. Names, characters, places, organizations and incidents are either products of the author's imagination or are used fictitiously. Any resemblance to actual events, organizations or persons, living or dead, is entirely coincidental.

All trademarks acknowledged.

This book is an original work of humour which makes comic reference to and draws parallels from a wide body of works including, but not limited to, those of JK Rowling. No endorsements or connections of any kind are claimed, nor should any be inferred.

Printed and bound in Great Britain by
Mackays of Chatham plc, Chatham, Kent

Cover illustration by
Steve Chadburn, www.cartoon.co.uk

Cover layout by
Kent Art Printers Ltd, Chatham, Kent

ISBN 0-9541568-0-3

Where permitted under the relevant local legislation, this book is sold subject to the condition that it shall not, by way of trade or otherwise, be lent, re-sold, hired out, or otherwise circulated without the publisher's prior consent in any form of binding or cover other than that in which it is published and without a similar condition including this condition being imposed on the subsequent purchaser.

*For Holly, one day we shall
write stories together*

Thanks To

Mark Towell, for his poetic contribution and for kicking around plot ideas with me in long alcohol-fuelled discussion; thanks also to Ian Porter for his critical insight.

CHAPTER 1

Parry was a long time waiting outside the headmaster's office. The school hadn't been able to reach his parents. They were in Stockholm to receive the inaugural Nobel Prize for Services to the Family, so a call had been made to Social Services instead.

The duty officer was going to be notified, and they would be sending someone to support Parry as soon as was possible. They helpfully added, "But don't hold your breath."

The police, however, had arrived promptly. It wasn't as if it was their first visit.

Parry sat opposite the policewoman.

Try as he might, he just couldn't get a decent fantasy going. She was not unattractive, stern looking, but not unattractive. She was wearing the uniform, and those black tights might have been stockings.

Her hair was tied back, ideal for those classic scenes where the female authority figure shakes loose her hair and becomes a teenage male's favourite fantasy figure, the experienced, beautiful and wanton woman.

She was even carrying handcuffs, so there was the whole bondage thing to explore. But still Parry just couldn't get his fantasy motivated.

Facing expulsion didn't help.

Nor did possible serious assault charges. Maybe, sexual assault charges.

He was still only fifteen. He might be put back into care.

Worse still, they might send him back to his foster parents. This is just the sort of thing they'd want to talk about for ages and ages and ages.

Parry thought about his options. He kind of hoped that the young offenders' institutions wouldn't be too full to take him.

It was the policeman, Constable Rodgers, who opened the headmaster's office door. He gently pushed Mike, the last of the witnesses to be informally interviewed, through the outer office where Parry sat, towards the corridor exit.

As he passed Parry, Mike grimaced and gave him a thumbs-down sign. To Parry's quietly mouthed 'piss-off', Mike mimed laughter and gave him a thumbs-up sign.

The policemen nodded at WPC Chapman. She stood and they both looked at Parry.

"Well lad, I think you'd better come in then," announced PC Rodgers.

Parry, prompted by WPC Chapman's hand on his shoulder, followed PC Rodgers into the office.

Dr Wendell, the headmaster, was looking curiously ill at ease. In the eight years he had been running the Ebbsfleet Community Comprehensive School, his short dark hair and dark complexion had both seemed to grey, though very little ever seemed to surprise him.

But right now, if Parry wasn't mistaken, the headmaster seemed a little rattled.

Miss Nicholls was there of course. She was wrapped in a raincoat and holding a mug of presumably sweet tea as if her life depended upon it. She looked both distressed and upset, quite the victim. She was supported by Miss Patterson, the sports teacher and, it had turned out, union rep. This rather explained the irritated science teacher, Mr Bradley, who had been kicking up and down the corridor like a spoilt child. For once he'd have nothing to do but go home early to his wife.

Constable Rodgers sat himself back down in the chair he had obviously been occupying for a while. He was close enough to the headmaster's large desk to rest his notebook on it as he wrote, and by his elbow an empty china teacup – alongside a few biscuit crumbs on the saucer and on the desk – testified to the traditional school office hospitality.

WPC Chapman manoeuvred Parry in front of the desk where both Dr Wendell and PC Rodgers could clearly see him. Parry pretty much had his back to his accuser, and WPC Chapman stood, probably deliberately, behind him and in front of Miss Nicholls.

"Now Parry," began Dr Wendell, "I don't want you to worry about the presence of these police officers. Constables Chapman and Rodgers are here responding to the alarm call. They are just sitting in, at my invitation, to understand the circumstances of the alarm. This isn't a police investigation, *at this stage*."

Parry clearly heard a snort from behind him.

"So son, in your own words, tell me what happened in detention this evening," instructed the headmaster.

"Dunno," stated Parry, looking at his shoes.

"Now come on man, we've heard from Sandra – Miss Nicholls," the headmaster corrected himself, "and we've heard from your schoolmates. Now I think it's time we heard from you."

"Dunno," restated Parry.

"You don't know what happened, or you don't know what to say?"

"Dunno."

"You don't know what, Parry?"

"Dunno."

"What don't you know, Parry?"

"What you just said."

Parry could almost hear the headmaster mentally counting to ten. Constable Rodgers snapped the lead of his clutch pencil, and was irritably clicking out another length.

The headmaster decided to try again. "What happened between you and Miss Nicholls?"

Parry thought about this for a moment. Feeling that a 'dunno' was probably not going to cut it this time, he fell back on a version of the truth.

"I never touched her."

"But you saw what happened?"

"Sort of."

"You were involved in what happened?"

"To Miss?"

"Yes, to Miss Nicholls. What did you do?"

"In detention?"
"Yes, in detention, tonight, between you and Miss Nicholls."
"Just now?"
"Yes."
"In detention?"
"Yes."
"Miss Nicholls?"
"Yes."
"Dunno sir. I never touched her, sir."

Dr Wendell started his silent counting again. The invitation to join the University of London as a full-time professor had sat quietly in his top drawer for a couple of days now. This evening had helped him to decide that he would much rather be discussing the theory of education than be involved in its grassroots practice.

Constable Rodgers drew thoughtful doodles on his notepad. He was a man of forty-eight years that felt like seventy. He was beginning to yearn for things to be relatively straightforward.

A person makes an accusation.

The accused makes a denial.

Statements are taken.

In general, the likeliest sounding story tends to be given credence. A warning given, or charges filed.

But that wasn't the story today.

Today, a teacher accuses a pupil of assault, but describes the incident as if the kid had never left his desk. The accused's most insightful statement so far had been 'I never touched her' – and the witnesses...

The constable thumbed through his notes.

Two lads heard and saw nothing. But that's not too unusual.

One girl claimed she saw everything, and swore blind that Parry attacked the teacher, but still places about half a football pitch between them during the alleged assault.

And then the accused's amigo swore blind that the teacher in question had a, quote, mental fit, unquote, and threw herself around the room as if possessed. He then recommended they call the Vatican to arrange an exorcism.

And they say television doesn't damage their minds.

Officer Rodgers supposed that Miss Nicholls might be suffering from stress.

He'd seen it often enough in the force. When decent people have to deal with scum all day, it can take its toll.

Perhaps ripping her clothes off in front of her class was this teacher's version of popping down to the cells and giving some luckless drunk a good kicking. A sign that some generous gardening leave is long overdue.

But how to deal with it, that was the problem.

There was a time, he remembered, when they'd take the kid down the station and scare the devil out of him. Maybe rough him up a bit.

Even if he wasn't exactly guilty of this current crime, he'd more than likely already have gone unpunished for several more serious ones. Taught them a little respect for their fellow man it did, being slapped around in the cells for a bit.

'If we treat yer like this when yer innocent,' we used to tell 'em, 'think how much worse it will be for yer if we ever catch yer guilty.'

Still, you couldn't do that anymore.

That was progress for you, the Constable thought bitterly.

Now the officer's biggest problem was extricating himself from the situation without having to write a report that had Miss Nicholls' name and the word 'nutter' in the same sentence.

The office door flew open.

"Coo-ee, I'm not too late am I? You're all so *quiet* in here, I thought you might have all gone home."

The newcomer sucked his bottom lip for a moment as he appraised the decor of the room. "Hate what you've done with this place, but still, each to their own I suppose."

It took a few moments for the assembly in the office to react to him. His white suit alone had a similar effect to the flash of a stun grenade tossed into the room.

Then he'd started talking.

Talking as if it were the most natural thing in the world for him to be there, and for them to be treated to his opinions. The newcomer's attention was drawn to the trophy cabinet.

"Oh, isn't this lovely," he said brightly, peering into the display case and flicking some dust off it with a peach hanky. "A concerto in Perspex and gilded plastic. Adds a little bit of kitsch to the room, don't you think? God knows it needs it."

Belatedly, the stranger seemed to notice everyone was staring at him.

"Oh don't mind me, I've come to collect..." – he wrinkled his nose when he first looked straight at Parry – "...him. You just carry on. I'll just take him when you've finished."

"Oh," said the headmaster, grabbing the only explanation that seemed reasonable to him, "you must be from Social Services."

"Yeeesss," said the newcomer, his finger on his chin as if he were considering the possibility, "you could say that. Oh my, that *poor* plant!"

The man in the white suit nipped around the back of the headmaster's desk, and began a sympathetic examination of a neglected pot plant.

"Mister, er, er?" fished the headmaster.

"Call me Gordon," said the man in the white suit, clearly pained by the state of the foliage. "Everybody does. You know, these need more light than this." Gordon pulled the plant away from the wall and adjusted the headmaster's curtains.

"And this is *so dry*," Gordon continued. "You know," he said, addressing the headmaster sternly, "you must never let it dry out like this."

Gordon plucked a teapot from a side table, checked the contents and, satisfied that it wasn't too hot, tipped the remaining tea onto the poorly plant.

"Ooh, teabags," said Gordon reproachfully. "They may be terribly convenient, but I find they're never the same, don't you?"

It was PC Rodgers who saved Dr Wendell from the awkward silence. "Are you willing to take custody of the lad, until such time as his parents can take responsibility, while we investigate the complaint made against him?"

"Of course," Gordon was back to his effervescent self. "I'd be delighted to look after the boy for you. It is, after all, why I'm here."

"Secure custody?" spat Miss Nicholls, barely able to contain her hatred.

"Oh yes dear, quite secure," Gordon seemed pleased himself. "I can quite honestly say I don't think he will be troubling you again."

Gordon began to steer Parry towards the door. Parry's shoulders automatically retracted from Gordon's hands, so much so that Gordon was able to guide him from the room without laying a finger on him.

WPC Chapman, seeing her charge being spirited away, had the presence of mind to say; "We'll need contact details, accommodation address, release forms signed..."

"Let's get that all done in the morning, shall we?" replied Gordon in a conversational manner. "I expect we've all had quite enough for one day, and there's still so much to do to get this one settled for the evening."

Chapman looked to Constable Rodgers for guidance. He just shrugged as if to say he couldn't be bothered, one way or the other. He just wanted the problem to go away.

"Toodle-pip," Gordon waved cheerio, "and *do* look after that plant properly," he said, addressing the headmaster. "I'll send you some plant food to perk it up a little."

The headmaster caught himself returning Gordon's wave as the door closed. He would have been more embarrassed, but he saw he wasn't the only one.

༺๏༻

The two police officers returned to their patrol car.

A busy-looking woman caught sight of them from a distance, and began advancing on them, frantically waving one arm in the air to attract their attention.

The constables paused by the car, Rodgers leaning on it as they waited for the woman to reach them.

"I suppose she'll be all right, that teacher," offered Constable Rodgers by way of conversation.

"I know she bloody well will be," replied WPC Chapman, her forthright tone taking Rodgers entirely by surprise. "I don't think she gave me a second look, but I recognised her right off from sixth-form college. She couldn't keep her clothes on then, the brassy tart. I reckon she's just got more than she bargained for with today's audience."

Rodgers raised an eyebrow, but wasn't able to pursue the matter further before the busy woman arrived.

She only stopped shaking her arm in the air when she was within fifteen paces of them. She fumbled inside her jacket for a moment before finding a photo identity card to brandish at the officers.

"Mrs Williams," she introduced herself. "From Ebbsfleet Social Services. I understand you've got the Hotter boy here for me?"

Parry had been expecting to be taken to the car park, but instead Gordon was marching him in the direction of town. This suited Parry, who imagined Gordon must have left his car on the road somewhere, because clear of the school it would be easier to make his getaway.

"Well thanks for everything," said Parry, "see you around sometime."

Parry nipped between two parked cars and sprinted across the road. He ran a little further up the street to the first side turning where he settled into a jog. As he reached the junction at the end of the short road he glanced back over his shoulder.

He wasn't even being followed.

Not being the world's fittest teenager, he was glad to drop back to a walk. He rounded the corner at the end of the road and relaxed a little more. His foster-parents would be back in a few days, and he had until then to come up with a really good story...

"I do so like to see young people take exercise, but I do think there's a time and a place, don't you?" Gordon stood leaning against a lamppost, folding up the newspaper he'd been reading and looking for all the world as though he had been waiting there all day.

Parry belted across the road, running so fast that he nearly missed the alley he was looking for. He shot down the alley that separated two pairs of semi-detached houses, running the length of the homes and then their gardens, before very nearly vaulting the pedestrian gate at the end of the alley.

Parry picked himself up and started jogging across the green open space. If Gordon had been following him in a car, he wouldn't be able to now.

Then it occurred to Parry that Social Services knew where he lived. He could probably run as fast he liked home, and still find Gordon waiting there for him.

Parry executed a forty-five degree change of direction. Darren's would be the best house to go to – he hadn't been involved – but Darren lived miles away. Mike, on the other hand, only lived ten or fifteen minutes this way.

"Would you care for a scone, or a fondant fancy?"

Parry stopped dead in his tracks. Afraid of what he might see, he turned around very slowly.

What he saw was a picnic.

How he could have been so blind as to run straight past it without noticing he didn't know.

But there it was.

A large picnic table with a predominantly yellow tartan cloth thrown over it.

There were two silver place settings. There were sandwiches – egg and cress, salmon pâté, cucumber – and there were scones, plain and fruited.

There was clotted cream and blackcurrant, apricot and strawberry conserves. There were two glasses and a jug of fruit juice. There was champagne on ice, in an ornate silver bucket. There was a tea service, including a little bowl with sugar lumps and little silver sugar tongs, something Parry had never before seen in real life.

There was a large flask of hot water which Gordon was pouring into a fine china teapot.

"I normally drink 'Lady Grey', but I thought you might be more of an 'English Breakfast' kind of a person, hmm?"

This time, fear propelled Parry's feet faster than they'd ever moved in his life. Somewhere in the back of his head a little alarm bell was ringing, but he was only actually listening to the adrenalin being pumped around his system.

Now he wasn't running to anywhere.

He was just running away from the lunatic with the cream tea. And the fondant fancies.

Parry reached the trees and began to follow the path that led to a small green pond. He wasn't on the path for more than twenty seconds before darting up the bank on his left and making for a gap in the fence familiar to all the local schoolboys. He climbed through and joined a pathway that ran alongside some houses. A minute or two later, he emerged by a main road, heading towards a large roundabout.

As Parry reached the roundabout he made for the pedestrian underpass. He had the choice of a long slope, or the stairs, which he took. At the bottom was a tunnel that led to an open-air space inside the roundabout, encompassed by tall graffiti clad walls. The traffic on the road itself rumbled past well above his head.

There were four other exits, apart from the way he had came. The paths met in the middle, dividing the space into pizza slices of earth, now topped with a little grass, weeds, builders' rubble and litter.

Parry reached the centre, arbitrarily picked the second path on his left and headed for the corresponding pedestrian tunnel. As he entered the tunnel, his foot caught on something and he fell, slamming heavily against the cracked pavement.

"I think you and I need a little chat," said Gordon, withdrawing his foot. "This could have been *so* much more civilised. Honestly, I was beginning to think you're avoiding me. A chap could get quite offended."

Parry slowly picked himself up off the ground. His knees and elbows had the kind of numbness that follows an injury and precedes painful swelling. At Gordon's beckoning he followed him back into the pizza slice open space where they could take advantage of the evening sunshine.

and the seamy side of magic

"I was going to say this over a cup of tea and a slice of cake, but I suppose this place is as good as any. Parry, you're coming with me. Do try to stop bleeding."

Gordon handed Parry a peach-coloured hanky to staunch the flow of blood from his nose.

"Head back," Gordon advised. "That's right. You and I, difficult as it may be to believe, have something in common. We have a certain talent. A talent which needs honing, developing, *educating*."

Parry stared at him blankly.

"Honestly, how hard *did* you fall? You don't think that woman's clothes fell off by accident do you? Unquestionably, you have some magical ability. Questionable taste, but unquestionably some magical ability.

"My job is to bring you back to Warthogs. The Warthog Approved School of Magic and Wizardry. There you'll learn to control your power. Master your abilities."

Gordon appraised Parry for a moment. "Or die trying."

"I'm going to wizarding school?" asked Parry, his shaken mind processing Gordon's words a little slowly.

"Well, you're going to *a* wizarding school, certainly. To tell you the truth, Warthogs is where most of the more difficult students are placed. We like a challenge."

"Or do what trying?" Parry was catching up.

"I never said it was going to be easy."

"Well, all things considered," said Parry, "I think I'll pass. I reckon I'll take my chances here. Learn as I go along."

"I'm sorry, that's just not going to be possible. It's my way, or... or you *really* don't want to know what the alternative is." Gordon pursed his lips as he stared at Parry. "Do I know you from somewhere?"

Parry's mind was still on other possible alternatives. He shook his head.

"Ever been to Brighton, Pink Shore Club?"

Parry shook his head again.

"LA? Fairielights?"

Parry shook his head vigorously.

"Strange. You do seem awfully familiar. Are you sure I don't know you from anywhere?"

Parry tried a new tactic. "You have speak to my foster parents," he said. "If I'm supposed to change schools, they'll want to know about it. They'll have to agree."

"Tell me, is there still some small part of your tiny little mind that really thinks I'm a social worker? If there is, I'm going to be quite disappointed."

This is it, thought Parry, I'm being abducted by a gay man. I'll probably spend the rest of my life chained in some basement somewhere, being visited by men with moustaches and peaked caps, my only solace being endless reruns of '*The Shawshank Redemption*'.

"Now, you can't go to school dressed like that. We're going to need to buy you a few things..."

Lederhosen, Parry shouldn't wonder.

"And you'll need all the right equipment, of course..."

Whips, chains, restraint harnesses...

"Now, let me see, it gets dark at what? Nine-thirty? Ten o'clock? And what time is it now, oh, it's nearly a quarter to seven already. We really must hurry, we've so much to buy, and so little time to buy it in. Fortunately I just adore shopping. You're in the hands of an expert."

Gordon's face momentarily wore a surprised expression. And then his eyes rolled up into his head and he fell forward like a plank, making no attempt to break his own fall. A trickle of blood had just begun to seep from the back of his injured head.

Parry dropped the brick, and made a hobble for it.

༺࿇༻

By the time Parry had almost reached home, a plan was forming in his mind.

He knew he had to get away. He didn't know where Gordon had come from, but clearly the man was deranged. Worse still, homosexual.

Possibly dangerous.

He should have just kept hitting him with the brick, he told himself.

But he did have a plan.

He had to get away, so his first thoughts had been to head for Reading. He'd been to the festival before now, and thought it must be a pretty cool place to hang out any time of year.

There was a tent in the loft, although he'd never actually put it up himself – Mike and Darren quite liked doing that sort of thing.

Then he vaguely remembered campsite toilet facilities.

He really wasn't sure he could face them sober.

Then Parry had a much better idea.

He had his passport at home. He had a fair amount of money in the bank, and he had his foster dad's charge card.

Or at least, he knew where it was hidden.

His foster parents were well-meaning people, a little on the soft side. With any luck they'd keep paying the charge card bills until he was at least eighteen.

Maybe twenty-one.

That was it then.

He'd go to Ibiza.

He could afford to stay in a pretty decent hotel while he sorted himself out and looked for a permanent pad.

He could have it large every night.

He might find some bar work. With a bit of luck he could live the Ibiza life.

That'd be a stroke.

Something to thank Gordon for.

Parry made a mental note to stay away from the gay quarter.

He'd get a bus into town, and train into London. There he could get a train to Gatwick. Or Heathrow.

He could be in Ibiza before Gordon knew what hit him.

Literally.

Convinced of his course of action, Parry turned the last corner into Primrose Drive. He was...

...not home.

This was not Primrose Drive.

Parry turned and looked back the way he'd come.

He stared for a very long moment at the grubby wall.

He touched it, just to make sure it was real.

Parry looked around.

He was in a blind alley.

From what he could see, and the traffic noise, he guessed he was in a large town or city.

There was a group of men at the other end of the alley, the exit end.

The word 'gang' sprung into Parry's mind. Immediately preceded by the word 'vicious'.

Then of course there was the pink tutu.

The pink tutu that Parry was wearing.

Parry sunk down behind a large plastic rubbish bin.

"So, it's come to this, has it?" asked Gordon.

Parry looked up and saw Gordon standing there with a scarf around his head to disguise his injury. "Beaten to death by an angry mob while wearing a pink tutu. I must say I am quite impressed in a way. You're going to be a martyr. People will remember your name for weeks and weeks, months, maybe years even. I shouldn't wonder if they turn your funeral into a Gay Pride parade."

Parry shook his head fearfully. "I'll tell them it's a joke. Fancy dress," he said uncertainly.

Gordon sucked his lips thoughtfully. "You know, I don't think that's going to work. Not only are those very angry people, but they had a bit of a set-to last night. They had parked their motorcycles outside 'The Pink Shore'. You know, I think they might have been looking for trouble, because they were getting really quite abusive towards some of the regulars. So I had a quiet word."

Gordon unwrapped the scarf from his head and looked at the bloodstain, touching himself gingerly behind his head. He snapped the scarf out and glanced at each side to check the bloodstain had gone, and then folded it neatly into his pocket.

"I made their motorbikes into a very interesting sculpture, set it on a traffic island where everybody could see it. I thought the twisted metal served as a powerful counterpoint to the vulnerability of their naked bodies. It looked so lovely 'til the

and the seamy side of magic

Fire Brigade came and cut them out of their bikes. You know, I was starting to believe that they weren't art lovers at all, with all the fuss they made.

"And of course the words 'Gay Pride' you've got tattooed across your forehead really aren't going to improve matters for you."

"Please," Parry was shaking with fear. This was no way for a young man to go, beaten to death in a pink dress.

"I'm sorry," said Gordon, "didn't I make myself clear? I suppose it was quite difficult with all that running from one place to another. And then being hit on the head with a brick. My job is to take you to the Warthog Approved School of Magic and Wizardry. Or you'll die while I'm trying."

"Why...what....?" enquired Parry incisively.

"Well, we can't let wizards and witches run around wild now can we? It causes all sorts of trouble. Trouble that I'll only have to sort out at one time or another. It's even more dangerous now than it used to be. Can you imagine the problems if some government got hold of one of us? There is a lot a wizard can do to defend himself, but there are only so many high velocity bullets you can dodge. Explosives can be very tricky. Particularly the thermonuclear ones. No, we really don't want to get into that. So we keep ourselves to ourselves.

"We've made some space for our kind adjacent to this muddled world. We can keep an eye on it, we can come and visit, but we really wouldn't want to live here. Now you could come with me. Or you could stay here. In spirit, anyway."

Parry sat trembling against the wall, his eyes fixed on the gang at the other end of the alley.

"I'll just give them a quick whistle then, shall I?" asked Gordon, bringing two fingers up to his mouth...

CHAPTER 2

The wall shimmered and became glasslike for a moment. Gordon and Parry stepped through. Parry wasn't immediately impressed. He was still in an alleyway. Not the same alleyway, but clearly an alleyway.

He looked down. The pink tutu had gone, he was in his own clothes again. That at least was an improvement.

He rubbed his forehead. He would really only be happy once he had seen a mirror, seen for himself that he had no tattoo.

Gordon got his bearings. "Ah, this way I think. Yes," he agreed with himself. Gordon went marching towards one end of the alley. This at least looked a little more promising. The alley opened out into a shopping precinct. The shops were modern, quite touristy, some a little avant-garde. Parry recognised it. He had visited it before – briefly. He was somewhere in London's West End.

"This way!" said Gordon brightly. He marched Parry up the road and paused in front of yet another alleyway between two buildings. "Will you look at that," Gordon said, glancing down towards his feet. Parry followed his gaze but all he saw was the stone paving.

"Look at what?" asked Parry.

"Oh, nothing." Gordon turned and led the way into the sex shop that now replaced the empty alleyway. This was just the sort of thing that Parry was afraid of.

There were a couple of people browsing in the first section of the shop, trying not to seem too interested in some of the items of leather clothing and raunchy underwear. But Gordon didn't dally. He walked straight through toward the back of the shop where it said '*Strictly Adults Only*'.

Parry followed him, not wanting to be either too close or too far behind. He reached the black curtained doorway and paused.

It did say '*Adults Only*' and technically…

and the seamy side of magic 27

An arm came through the curtain, grabbed Parry by the collar and pulled him through. "There now," said Gordon, "that wasn't so bad, was it?"

Parry looked around. Here were displayed a great many interesting magazines which no doubt could even put Mike's brother's collection to shame. Suddenly spending some time here didn't seem like such a bad idea, but Gordon led him further into the back of the shop.

They passed handcuffs, restraint devices and the type of clothing designed to expose the parts normally concealed, and conceal the parts normally exposed. Whips, chains and harnesses – not to mention toys of every shape, colour and variety – decorated the walls. Some of them were enough to make a chap feel quite inadequate.

As if by magic, the shopkeeper appeared.

A portly man wearing waistcoat and fez, the shopkeeper beamed at Gordon. "Delighted to see you again sir, what manner of adventure may I introduce to you today?"

"Sadly Omar, I have no time to play today. Two to Xfordo Reetsti, if you would be so kind."

"Of course." The shopkeeper took two cloaks from a rack by his side and presented them to Gordon, who accepted with a polite nod of his head.

Gordon glanced at his watch. "We must hurry," he said, "we haven't much time." He put one hand behind Parry and firmly pushed him into a changing room and followed him in. Parry almost froze with horror. He couldn't imagine what was about to happen.

"Oh don't flatter yourself!" Gordon draped a cloak around Parry and the other around himself. "Honestly! You're really not at all my type." He grabbed the cubicle curtain and pulled it sharply open.

There was a shopping street, but nothing like Parry had ever seen before. The buildings looked as though each had been placed individually in the road, some a bit further forward, others further back, some made of wood, some of stone, some of brick and some of materials Parry couldn't even guess at. The road was narrow and cobbled, designed it seemed for pedestrian use rather than heavy traffic. And the people – well, the people just weren't normal, were they?

On the whole, people here wore dresses. Men and women alike. As it was now getting late, some wore capes as well. Although he had to admit the chaps weren't wearing very girlie dresses and most of the girls' dresses weren't very girlie either. They tended to be made of strong solid materials, material that looked as though it would be hardwearing, warm if it had to be, possibly waterproof. The cuffs on the dresses tended to be very wide and people seemed to be able to store all manner of things up their sleeves. Or if it was cold, hands could simply disappear completely, each tucked into the opposite sleeve.

It was something like a cross between the robes Friar Tuck had worn in a Robin Hood film and the outfits Parry had seen on Shaolin monks when they came to perform their Kung Fu stage show. Hats, if worn, tended to be tall and pointed; a few sagged and the points trailed down individuals' backs. Some of the clothes looked as if the wearer had owned them for a thousand years.

The people themselves were fairly remarkable; they were all shapes and sizes, from dwarf to giant, and there was every colour of skin, including several which you wouldn't see at the United Nations. Particularly blue. And green.

The shops displayed their wares both in their windows and in the street in front of them. Big cooking pots, little cooking pots, things to stir with, and things to poke fires. Parry looked up at the name of the shop. It announced itself as *The Fancy Cauldron*. Outside the next shop there were brooms. There were all sorts of brooms there to be fair, but it did seem to specialise in the type of broom that had a bundle of brushwood at one end.

Witches' brooms, thought Parry.

"First," said Gordon, "you'll need a wand."

"A wand?" Parry asked automatically.

"Of course you need a wand," said Gordon, leading the way past a shop that seemed to be selling parts that belonged inside one creature or another. Parry found walking easier if he didn't try and guess where they'd come from. "A wand channels your magical energies," said Gordon. "Otherwise the results can be unfocused. Unpredictable. You have to be a very fine wizard indeed not to use a wand. You'll like having a wand," he said. "Boys your age love to have a little tool to play with."

Gordon led the way into one of the many little shops. The proprietor's face lit up with recognition as Gordon entered, and then fell again as he saw the individual who was following him.

"It's lovely to see you again sir! Always a pleasure. How may we help you today?" Gordon was clearly a favourite among the shopkeeping fraternity.

"Albert," greeted Gordon. "So nice to see you. But we need a wand for this chap in a little bit of a hurry."

"Of course, sir, we'll see what we can find," said Albert, all smiles at Gordon. His face returned to its dour self as he looked at Parry. "I wonder what would suit sir."

Parry was amazed. Stacked around him in this tiny little shop were wands displayed as a jeweller might display them. Most were in glass cases arranged on little stands or velvet cushions. Some were locked in cases and cabinets at the back of the room, one or two slowly revolved under glass domes without any apparent means of support. "I am sure we'll find sir a wand that will meet with his satisfaction. Although of course, it's really the wand that chooses the person."

"This is…" Albert picked a wand off the shelf. He swung it from side to side – "a very fine piece. Did you have a price range in mind, sir?"

Gordon glanced at Parry and then back to Albert. He wrinkled his face up a little and holding one hand at hip height indicated a very small distance using his thumb and forefinger.

Albert looked at Gordon, then at Parry, and then back to Gordon. "I see, sir. I quite understand."

He placed the wand back on its velvet cushion, bent down behind the counter and pulled out a large wooden box. He dumped it on the table. "Let's see what we have in here." He grabbed a handful of wands, placed them on the top of the counter and straightened them out. "Come here lad," he told Parry. "We can't try them out without you, now can we?"

Parry walked over. He picked a long black rod from amongst the wands and gave it a trial wave or two in the air. Albert regarded him suspiciously and snatched the wand out of his fingers.

"Perhaps sir is unfamiliar with how we select a wand?"

Parry stared at Albert for a few moments and then glanced at Gordon. Parry didn't have time to say anything before there was a sharp stinging sensation across his left cheek and jaw.

"No. That one won't do." Albert dropped the black wand back into the box and selected another. Just as the word 'ow' was forming in Parry's mouth, Albert slapped him across the other cheek with the second wand.

"Ow, ow!" objected Parry.

"Not that one either," said Albert, dropping it back into the case. He took the next one.

Parry took a huge step backwards. "Are you bonkers?" Parry felt one hand being caught and his arm twisted behind his back as Gordon forced him back to the counter.

"I'm sorry," said Gordon to Albert. "He's new. Wasn't brought up to our ways." The man behind the counter nodded, looked at Parry and then slapped him across the face with the next wand, and then the next, and the next. He'd pick up each wand and inspect it closely. If it were imperfect in any way he would toss it back into the case. If it were fine, he would slap it across Parry's face.

"What the hell are you doing?" demanded Parry.

"We're just trying to find a wand that suits you," explained Gordon. "Not an easy task by any means."

"So why am I being beaten around the face? Ow!" said Parry as another wand struck him.

"We need to find one that resonates with your individual character and personality."

"Ow!" said Parry to the next slap. "And smacking me in the face helps, does it?"

"You'll know when it's right," Gordon told him. This time the wand hit Parry and his head spun, his body following a few moments after. He twisted in mid-air for a few seconds, before his body got the idea that it could use the momentum for travel, and he was flung across the room. Parry hit hard into the corner between a display cabinet and the front window, and sank slowly to the floor.

"MDF, melamine veneer, fibre optic core," read Albert from the wand's label. "Slight second."

"That'll do nicely," said Gordon. "How much?"

"That'll be two half-crowns," said Albert.

"Certainly. Lovely!" said Gordon, proffering a gold coin.

Albert took the money. "A crown, sir, very good." He opened an old fashioned mechanical till and returned two silver coins to Gordon. "Will there be anything else?"

"Not today," said Gordon. "In a bit of a rush."

Still shaken, Parry picked himself up off the floor.

Gordon wished farewell to Albert and caught Parry by the sleeve, taking him out onto the street. "At least we've got the most essential item," said Gordon, "but I think we'll need to split up to have any chance of getting the rest this evening."

Gordon pushed Parry against the wall and straightened him up a little. He glanced up and down the road, concerned at the loss of light. Taking a small drawstring purse from his pocket he fished out a couple of gold coins and handed them to Parry. Splitting up with Gordon didn't exactly upset Parry, especially if Gordon was going to give him money to fund his getaway.

"Now listen," said Gordon. "There are a hundred and forty-four pieces in a crown. Those are two one-crown coins I've given you. Now watch your change because there are only thirty-six pieces, that's three bits, in half-a-crown – yes? So four silver half-crowns to a golden crown. Now there are sixty crowns in a chest, twenty-four chests in a trove and thirteen troves in a galleon. Not that you are likely to see that much money. Have you got that?"

Parry was still concentrating on the fact he was holding two gold coins. "Got it!" he lied.

"I'm going to go and get your supplies, books and ingredients and such, but you will have to go and collect your uniform – you need to do that in person," said Gordon. "Do you understand?"

Parry was looking at his two gold coins. "Yes," he said automatically, quite disconnected from anything Gordon was saying.

Gordon shook him by the shoulders. "Uniform – you go down that way." He pointed down the street, but Parry was still staring at the coins. He took Parry's head and twisted it in the right direction. "How hard did that wand hit you? The uniform shop is down that way," he told Parry. "Second alley on the right – have you got that?"

"Right," said Parry. "Second alley."

"It's called Threads," said Gordon. "Even you should be able to remember that. Tell them its Warthogs school fifth year," instructed Gordon. "And do hurry! You don't want to end up going in what you're wearing, do you?"

Parry shook his head, largely because that's what he imagined Gordon to want.

Gordon stared at him for a moment, shook his own head, then turned on his heels and made off in the opposite direction from that in which he had pointed Parry.

Parry looked up and down the road – all those shops he really didn't want to look in involved bits and pieces of animal; sometimes bats, sometimes lizards, but often things that he couldn't even imagine, but there were more interesting shops. Some had telescopes and star charts. Some had interesting stones covered in a language he didn't understand. Some had huge staffs and great robes that he imagined a powerful wizard would wear. There were a surprising number of shops selling frilly shirts. Parry guessed it must be fashionable.

He made his way up the road. As hungry as he was he daren't approach many of the food stalls. There was very little food there that he actually recognised and he really didn't fancy his chances of picking something that wasn't going to be completely revolting. But there was one trader selling something he seemed to recognise. Parry approached him, joining a small queue who were collecting the bags of roast goodies. "Are they chestnuts?" Parry asked the vendor.

The vendor wore a heavy cloth hat and a heavily singed robe. He looked down at the brazier and poked the contents thoughtfully for a few moments. "Could be," he replied. "Could be chestnuts, I suppose."

Parry looked at the vendor for a few moments. He noticed what looked like blood amongst the burns on his robe, then he looked behind the trader. There was a small furry pile of rats' heads over to one side. On the other side of the vendor there was a broken pile of very small skulls. Parry's stomach jumped into his mouth. He stepped away, and then further away, and then ran.

The vendor watched Parry's flight as he tipped over display baskets and barged through the crowd. "Huh!" he shook his head. "Tourists!"

Parry was catching his breath. He was in the space between two of the ramshackle buildings, a few doors down from where the buildings had all been stone and marble. He thought he was fairly safe for a few moments.

He listened to the noises of the market until two voices caught his interest above all else.

"Stir your cauldron, luv?" came the lecherous invitation.

"Just what kind of a girl do you think I am?" a stout girl of around Parry's age was demanding of a heavily-built blonde boy whose face looked fixed in a wicked expression – as if he had been enjoying evil pleasures when the wind changed.

"Oh come on Jude – what's your problem?" the boy asked.

"Look! Will you just get away from me!"

"I've got money!"

The girl stopped in her tracks. She didn't actually turn round but she looked thoughtful. "Look!" said the lad again – "a one bit piece." He held up a coin pressed between his stubby thumb and forefinger. The girl turned round. She stared at the coin for a few moments and then at the boy. She reached for the coin but he whipped it away and held it behind his head. "Not until after," he said.

She stared at him for a few moments. "Just a kiss?"

"All right, all right. No funny stuff!" said the lad. "Just a kiss."

The girl was staring at the coin. "A one bit piece," the lad reminded her.

The girl looked up and down the road as if checking to see there was no one she knew. "Oh, alright Freddie. Quickly then," she agreed.

The boy embraced her and pushed his mouth onto hers. The girl's arms, which had been hanging by her sides, slowly came up as she waited to be released. She tapped the boy on the arm, then she poked him, then using both hands started to peel his face from hers. With a sudden movement the boy grabbed the girl's bum in one hand and her breast with the other. Her knee came up with a vicious and practised accuracy. The boy collapsed almost in slow motion. His face revealed both pain and a great deal of amusement.

The girl snatched the coin from where it fell. "It's clipped!" she screamed.

"Well you're not perfect either!" said the boy from his knees, only to receive a parting kick to his leg.

"I saw it all!" said Parry. "Nice moves." He hauled the lad up on to his feet. Quite a job, because although he didn't have Parry's height, he was a thickly-built boy, solid muscle.

"Thanks," said Freddie.

"I'm Parry."

"All right, Parry?" He looked Parry up and down as if he were wearing some sort of fancy dress. "I'm Frederick Weasel," he said. "Call me Freddie. Fancy a frothy one?"

Parry had no idea what a frothy one was. So of course he said that he fancied one.

"In here then," said Freddie, leading Parry into what in other circumstances might have been described as a café. Ahead of them the girl Freddie had called Jude was arguing with the chap behind the counter. A large steaming mug sat in front of her with a few small coins next to it.

"It's not that clipped!" Jude was shouting.

"Take it or leave it!" The guy behind the counter clearly wasn't in a mood to argue. The girl stamped her foot – a minor event on the Richter scale – and snatched up the drink and the coins and sat herself at a table. This seemed to amuse Freddie. Walking up to the bar Freddie ordered two large frothy ones. "Eight pieces," the chap behind the counter said.

"Bit brassic at the minute," Freddie said to Parry, nodding towards Jude. Parry woke up and got the idea. He fished out one of the two coins that Gordon had given him and placed it in front of the barman. The barman raised an eyebrow.

"You want change, do you?"

Freddie saw the coin. "Bloody right he does!"

The chap slid the coin off the counter, inspected it for a few moments and then dropped it into his open till. The barman stuck two large mugs on the counter and then a pile of coins. A couple of small brown coins, five coins Parry recognised as bits that Freddie had been trying to buy the girl off with and two larger silver coins. Each of the bits had a triangle cut from the coin, looking like a pizza slice had been taken from it.

"They're clipped!" accused Parry, making an educated guess. The guy behind the bar just stared at him for a few moments.

"Take it or leave it," the barman said, but as Freddie had already collected the drinks and was placing them down on the table the girl had found for herself, Parry thought it would be better to take it. He wasn't sure that getting into an argument in a place like this would be entirely healthy. Parry slid the coins off the counter and stuck them in his pocket and went to catch up with the other two.

"This is my mate Parry," Freddie introduced him. It seemed buying Freddie a drink was enough to get into matesville. The girl seemed to be trying to ignore Freddie, but acknowledged Parry.

"Judicita Harmonica," the girl said, extending one hand.

It took Parry a few moments to realize the collection of syllables was her name.

"Jude to my friends," she told him, withdrawing the hand that Parry was ignoring.

"But as she doesn't have any friends," said Freddie, "the rest of us call her 'Hormoany'." This was good enough for Parry, who immediately began to think of the girl as 'Hormoany' rather than 'Jude' or 'Judicita'.

'Hormoany' shot Freddie a poisonous look but Freddie didn't care. He lifted up his mug. "Cheers, Parry," he said, and took a long swig.

Parry lifted his mug and gingerly took a sip. "What's in it?" he asked.

Freddie looked at him for a moment, looked at his clothes and said, "You've not been here long."

"Arrived today," confirmed Parry.

"I see," said Freddie. "Best you don't know then, might put you off, stop you enjoying it. Cheers!" he said again and took another swig. To Parry the liquid seemed fairly palatable, spicy, perhaps a bit of ginger in there, but it was all right.

"So where are you from?" asked Freddie.

"Ebbsfleet," said Parry, trying to identify what had floated to the top of his mug.

"From where?" asked Hormoany.

"Ebbsfleet," said Parry. "In Kent."

"Kent?" asked Freddie.

"Yeah," said Parry, "Kent, England, Earth."

Hormoany and Freddie looked at one another. Then a little realization dawned. "Oh, we mean where in the magical world?"

"I don't know what you mean," said Parry.

"Where did you grow up? What school do you go to?"

"In Ebbsfleet," said Parry. "You know, where the train station is, the Channel Tunnel. I went to Ebbsfleet Comprehensive, 'til today when I was abducted."

"You mean you actually grew up in the real world?" said Hormoany, amazed.

"I haven't even been allowed to visit," complained Freddie.

"Well, not since you blew up the dorm anyway," commented Hormoany.

"It must be really cool, living there. You've got flat screens everywhere in the real world," enthused Freddie. "That's so much better than staring into a crystal ball all the time."

Parry looked at him. "Suppose."

"You could always use a mirror, if you don't like crystal balls," Hormoany told Freddie haughtily.

"Mirrors got opinions. Never trust a screen with its own opinion about what it wants to show you."

and the seamy side of magic

"So what are you doing here then?" Hormoany asked Parry. "Most... most non-magical people, can't get here. And if they did, well..." She shook her head and stared into her drink as if the consequences weren't going to be good.

"I was abducted," Parry reminded them. "Apparently I've got some magic in me so I've got to go to some school."

"What school?" asked Freddie.

"Warthogs," said Parry. "That's what he told me."

"Really! We go to Warthogs," Hormoany told him. She and Freddie both seemed to relax a little.

"So who brought you here?" Parry asked.

"My parents brought me," Hormoany replied. "But they always insist on travelling by broom though... it's *freezing* when you fly up into these mountains."

"Mountains?" wondered Parry, taken by surprise.

"I'm here with my brothers," said Freddie. "They're in the upper sixth year. Which year are you in?"

Parry thought for a moment. "Fifth," he said. "That's what he told me."

"Great! That means you'll be in with us. The fifth year is where the real fun stuff starts. We get to use wands, levitate stuff, change stuff into stuff, destroy stuff. It's cool."

"We also learn about healing, fertility, foretelling the future, working magics in harmony with nature..." added Hormoany.

"Yeah, but that's witchcraft. Girly stuff. I'm not doing any more of that than I have to," declared Freddie. "What house are you in?"

"Dunno," said Parry.

"We're in Sade House," Freddie informed him. "That's the coolest. You should try and be in that one, we have loads of fun."

"So who brought you here?" asked Hormoany.

"Some ponce in a white suit," said Parry miserably. He had fished something out of the top of his drink and was now trying to blow the froth off to get a good look at it.

"Blonde hair?" asked Freddie. "A bit girly?"

"Good with plants?" asked Hormoany.

"What – you know him?" asked Parry.

"Sounds like Gordon," said Freddie. "He's the Warthogs gardener."

"He's been at Warthogs like forever," said Hormoany. "Some say he came with Bol d'Areth, he might even be as old as Bol d'Areth."

"Don't be stupid," said Freddie. "Nobody is as old as Bol d'Areth, Bol d'Areth always likes to make sure of that."

Parry got round to asking the obvious question – "So who's Bol d'Areth?"

"You really haven't been here very long have you? He's a legend," said Hormoany.

"He's a pain in the neck," said Freddie.

"Bol d'Areth established the New Order when he stopped the Mage Wars," informed Hormoany. "That was the big war between all the most powerful wizards."

"He stopped a magical *war*?"

"Well, it's tough to keep a war going when you run out of participants," commented Freddie.

"He only killed evil wizards," said Hormoany.

"That's not what my great grandfather said," Freddie told Parry.

"What did he say?" Parry asked.

"I think his last words went something like... 'Die Bol d'Areth...argh!'"

"Ah," said Parry.

"Well it was his own stupid fault," Hormoany told Freddie. "Everyone knows no one can kill Bol d'Areth."

"Well everybody knows that now. The point is, they didn't know *then*," pointed out Freddie. "That's generally how you discover these things. You have a crack at killing someone, he survives a couple of dozen attempts then they give up trying. My great granddad was only at about attempt twelve. That was at the point where they reckoned if you wanted to do him in, you'd need to bring your biggest power staff and a few of your mates."

"So, where are your mum and dad?" Hormoany asked Parry in an attempt to change the subject.

and the seamy side of magic

"Well my foster parents – back in England – well they are probably back in England by now. They were in Stockholm."

"Where?" asked Freddie.

"That's in the real world," said Hormoany.

"Oh," said Freddie.

"What happened to your real parents?" asked Hormoany.

"Don't know," said Parry. "I was left at hospital, when I was newborn."

"Oh I get it," said Freddie, a dirty smile creeping over his face. "Some wizard pops out into the real world, has a bit of hanky panky, he disappears and some poor bird is left holding the baby!"

"You're disgusting!" snapped Hormoany.

"Happens all the time!" said Freddie.

"All right Freddie!" came a booming voice. "How you doing?"

"All right Jude?"

Parry looked up. Two very large men were either side of the table. They looked a lot like Freddie. They had the same kind of Neanderthal brow and their eyes shared the same wicked intelligence that Parry saw in Freddie.

If anything they were built heavier. A couple of extra years had piled on the pounds. Huge muscles hung on a very solid frame. These people were like tanks and they were very like each other – twins.

"This is Damian and Hannibal," Freddie introduced them. "My brothers," as if it needed saying. They sat down at the table, the benches creaking as they took the extra load.

"All right are you?" asked Hannibal.

"Who's your friend?" asked Damian.

"This is Parry."

Parry nodded. "Parry Hotter," he told them.

"That's interesting kit you're wearing."

"Oh, this?" Parry looked down at his blazer and trousers. "I've got to get some new stuff."

"We could help you out," suggested Damian.

"Always willing to oblige," nodded Hannibal.

"Excuse me," said Hormoany, shuffling off the edge of her bench. She looked around and then started heading for the conveniences located at the very back of the café. Freddie wriggled out too.

"Hold on Jude!" he called out to Hormoany. "Look what I've found! I've got half-a-crown!"

"Thought you said you were brassic," accused Parry.

"Oh I was! I found it," Freddie told him.

"Oh right," said Parry.

"In your pocket," completed Freddie. "Cheers mate!" He chased off in the direction that Hormoany had gone.

Parry felt a bit uncomfortable. He was sitting here with these two ogres of men he didn't really know. Still, he was friends with Freddie and these were his brothers. They weren't likely to do anything. Were they?

"Interesting togs," said Hannibal, leaning over to feel Parry's jacket.

"Don't see clothes like that around here very often," said Damian. "They look like other world clothes to me."

"Yeah, have you been visiting the other world?"

"It's where I come from," said Parry. "Just been dragged here by a guy called Gordon. Maybe you've heard of him?"

The brothers glanced at each other. Gordon's name had raised an eyebrow on each of them.

"So you're a foundling," said Damian.

"A magical kid found in the other world," clarified Hannibal.

"I suppose," supposed Parry.

"So you are going to need kitting out," said Hannibal.

"We can help," reassured Damian.

"Gordon said he's getting my stuff for me."

The brothers looked at one another and then back at him.

"He might get the ordinary stuff," conceded Hannibal.

"But he's hardly likely to spring for the good stuff," said Damian.

"The stuff you really need at school," said Hannibal.

"I mean, if you've only just come from the other world, you're going to need to do some catching up. We've got books that read themselves to you." Damian produced a little volume from one of his pockets. He flicked through the pages and Parry could hear the whispering as he did so.

"Or you might like a quill that knows how to write essays," said Hannibal, producing a tatty-looking feather which immediately started scratching away across the desk.

"Needs ink," said Hannibal, stating the obvious.

"What I really need," Parry told them, "is some way of getting out of here, getting away from Gordon."

The boys thought about this for a moment. "Escape is it? Not easy to escape from somebody like Gordon. A broom would help – a flying broom. Or a flying carpet."

"Pricey," said Hannibal.

"Pricey," agreed Damian.

"But what if," said Hannibal as an idea occurred to him, "we were to give this lad the Stone of Ekoms."

"That's powerful magic," said Damian. "Are you sure we should entrust it to a novice?"

"It *is* powerful," acknowledged Hannibal, "but if he needs to get away from somebody like Gordon…"

"Gordon. Gordon, Gordon, Gordon," tutted Damian. "I feel sorry for the lad. What do you reckon?"

"Well, he looks like someone who knows what he's doing. I think we might be able to trust him with it."

"Tell me," Damian said to Parry. "Would you like to be able to become invisible?"

"Yes," said Parry. That could be the answer, he was thinking. He imagined being able to slip past Gordon. But then think of the possibilities. So many bedrooms, so little chance of being caught.

Then he remembered the Invisible Man films he had seen. "Don't have to be naked, do I?" he asked.

The brothers seemed slightly puzzled. "Only if you want to be," replied Hannibal.

"Now the Stone of Ekoms isn't an everyday item," said Damian.

"Very exclusive indeed," said Hannibal.

"We can't let it go to just anyone, but he *is* a friend of Freddie's," said Damian.

"Well, I suppose to a very good friend of Freddie," agreed Hannibal.

"Do you have some consideration?" asked Damian.

Parry looked blank.

"Some tokens of exchange," hinted Hannibal.

"Hard cash," clarified Damian.

"Money?" realized Parry. "Yes, I've got some money." He emptied his pocketful of coins onto the table. "How's this?"

Damian seemed thoughtful. "So how much have you got there?"

"I don't know," said Parry. "Look, I've got a gold coin and silver ones and some of these bit things."

"New to the money?" asked Hannibal.

Parry looked up at him.

"Good job you ran into us," said Damian.

"There are those, you know," said Hannibal, looking at his brother, "who might take advantage of somebody in your situation."

"Very fortunate," his brother agreed, "that you ran into us." Damian produced a grey faceted stone from his pocket. It had runes and symbols running around its conical edge. "This," he said, "is the Stone of Ekoms."

"Invisibility can be yours," promised Hannibal.

"Let's just see what we've got here, shall we," said Damian, using one finger to spread the coins out on the table. "Now, see here, we've got a couple of half-crowns. Of course they're not worth half-a-crown. Oh no! A half-crown isn't worth half-a-crown, dear me no! We've got a few bits here, we've got a gold crown – that's two dozen pieces for a gold crown – of course the exchange rate – oh yes the exchange rate –"

"– fortunately is very much in your favour, young man," said Hannibal.

"Oh very much in your favour," agreed Damian. The gold coin slipped off the table and was replaced by an assortment of tokens including a number of red triangular coins.

"Half a dozen ickstran to a crown now," Hannibal told Parry.

"That's very good," said Damian. "Not being too generous are you?"

"Not at all!" said Hannibal. "It is a friend of Freddie's, after all. Now let's see – half-crown – worth a dozen pieces here and these five bits come to one piece. He slipped Parry's coins off the table and dropped others in their place. "Of course, once exchanged into ubbishray we can exchange it for the Stone." Hannibal leant towards Parry. "You know the Stone must be purchased with ubbishray, don't you?" Parry, who knew nothing about anything here, just nodded.

"So, we can now do business," said Damian collecting back half the unusual coins on the table and placing the Stone in front of Parry. "But don't tell anyone we were so generous."

"We don't want to lose our reputation, now do we, Damian?"

The brothers glanced over their shoulders at the sound of an injured Freddie falling against a wall, laughing in his pain. Judicita Harmonica pushed past him.

"Time we were going," announced Hannibal.

"Good doing business with you," Damian told Parry. "All transactions are binding. No Refunds. No recourse."

"I'd put all that money away if I were you," suggested Hannibal. "Don't want to leave such value hanging around."

"You'll create the cloak of invisibility by running your fingers around the runes," whispered Damian.

"But don't try it in here," cautioned Hannibal. "It might be a bit obvious, and then everyone would be after getting it off you." The brothers got up from the table and made their way to the door.

Parry was just quick enough to get the coins and the Stone in his pocket before Freddie and Hormoany returned to the table.

"Oh that hurt!" said Freddie, clearly amused. "I just wish I could say it was worth it."

"You sod," said Hormoany.

Freddie drained his drink. "Fancy another?" he asked Parry. "Hormoany is buying."

Hormoany was putting Parry's silver half-crown into her purse.

"No, I'm certainly not," she stated firmly. "Anyway, it's late. I told my parents I would meet them when the shops started to shut."

"Already?" exclaimed Parry. "I still need to get my uniform."

"Fair enough," said Freddie as the three of them got up from the table. "Catch you another time – yeah?"

They wandered down between the witches and wizards and various magical species that inhabited the bar. As they reached the door a wizard pushed past them. He caught himself short, grabbing his stomach. He turned and flicked a hand out, catching Freddie around the ear. "Be more careful where you are going, boy," the wizard snapped.

"Ouch," said Freddie, more to himself than anybody.

"Do you know him?" asked Parry.

"Oh that was Jape," said Freddie – "he's a teacher at Warthogs. Miserable old sod! Anyway," – pointing to an alleyway across the road – "that's where you want. That's where you'll find Threads. See you at school tomorrow?"

"Suppose," said Parry – his hand on the Stone in his pocket – 'Unless,' he thought, 'I can get away before then.'

Parry crossed the road. Looking down the lane he saw amongst two or three shops the sign he was looking for – Threads.

A thin woman about forty-five or fifty years old sat outside the shop, rocking to and fro on a stool. She wore a money belt around her waist and a short apron with a pole through the bottom edge. She seemed to wake up as Parry began his march down the street. Glancing up at the clock hanging outside the shop, she stood up, collected her stool and the little sign that read '*Robemakers to Sorcerers since 30820*' and stepped inside her store.

As Parry got there she shut the door and, looking him in the eye, turned the sign from '*Open*' to '*Closed*'.

A small sandy-haired boy with round glasses arrived at the shop a moment or two after Parry. He saw the closed signed but waved vigorously at the proprietor before she had time to turn away. He lifted up a piece of parchment and held it against the window for a few moments. The woman read it and, with clearly discernible irritation, opened the door again.

and the seamy side of magic

The small lad slipped through. The woman pushed the door, but it caught on Parry's foot. She stared at him for a few moments and then, as if she really couldn't care less, released the door and allowed Parry to follow the young lad in.

The seamstress relieved the child of his parchment – "One Warthogs uniform, made to measure, for collection today. Name of Deux-Pantoufles."

She walked over to the shelves, most of which were empty, selected a small pile of clothing and lifted it down to the main counter. She unfolded one or two items and held them against the child; a robe, a shirt with long tails. "Yes," she said, "these are the goods."

The seamstress folded them up and placed them in a stiff cardboard bag. "One and two half-crowns," she said. The boy gave her a couple of gold coins like those Gordon had given Parry. She moved behind the counter. Parry heard the rattle of the moneybox and she returned two silver coins to the boy. She turned to look at Parry. "Do you have an order?"

"I need a uniform," said Parry. "Warthogs."

"Everyone needs a Warthog uniform today. Have you," she repeated irritably, "got an order?"

"No," said Parry miserably.

The boy carrying his brand new clothes looked between the two of them and whispered to Parry, "Money talks, you know."

For a few moments Parry was going to take this literally. After all, he had seen a whispering book and a quill that wrote for itself, not to mention a number of other strange sights today. He could quite well believe that he could have a conversation with cash at this moment.

The small boy twitched his head a couple of times towards the woman behind the counter and Parry realized what he meant. He fished in his pocket and dropped his coins onto the counter, the heap of coins he had collected in change when he had purchased his Stone.

The woman sighed in a short sharp way. She huffed, and started separating out the coins into several distinct piles. "These," she said, "aren't legal tender anymore. These aren't legal tender in this country." Another pile. "These aren't legal tender in their own country anymore and these," – indicating the most valuable of the coins that Parry had received from the two brothers – "these" she said, "are tokens for a tavern slot machine."

There was a small pile of brown coins which the seamstress slipped into her hand and dropped into the unseen moneybox. She stepped into a back room for a few seconds and then was straight out. "This is what you can have for that."

She handed Parry a blazer badge. It had the word 'Warthog' written across four distinct emblems: it showed a king in front of some waves and another crowned figure by a golden girl, a man carrying an archers bow and a woman carrying a whip.

Still staring at the tiny badge he had received in consideration for all his worldly fortune, Parry was able to offer no resistance as the woman forcefully pushed him through the door. He came back to his senses to bang on the door and shout "My money! Give me back my money!" The door remained unanswered for a few moments, then it opened sharply and a shower of worthless coins bounced off Parry and onto the ground.

"Hello sir!" called the blonde-haired boy. "Nice to see you again, sir."

Gordon's distinctive voice came back, "Oh, Goodie – Goodie Deux-Pantoufles isn't it? How's your brother Martin?"

"He's well sir."

"And your mother?"

"She's very well sir, thank you sir."

"And your father?"

"He'd like you to stay away from Martin, sir."

"Oh," said Gordon. "I see."

"Looking forward to starting school again tomorrow sir. I'll be starting the fifth year. Get to learn some real magic. I'm especially looking forward to learning the arts of witchcraft. So much more ecologically sound than so much of the magic taught to wizards, don't you think sir?"

"I'm sure," said Gordon noncommittally, "and I see you've met one of the new boys." Goodie glanced at Parry sitting dejectedly on the floor.

"Yes sir. I look forward to your horticulture lessons sir," said Goodie, almost saluting a good-bye.

"Yes," said Gordon. "I'm sure you do."

Gordon was weighed down with bags and books. He looked at Parry who was collecting the coins off the ground. "Where's your uniform?" Gordon asked.

"She wouldn't sell me one," said Parry. "It's her fault! She threw my money on the ground!"

Gordon looked at the motley collection of coins Parry was picking up. "Where did you get all that rubbish?" he asked.

"Well, I met this guy Freddie and his brothers."

"Weasel? Freddie Weasel? You met the Weasel Brothers?"

Parry looked up. "Yeah."

Gordon rolled his eyes. "I can't leave you alone for two minutes. Well, you're just going to have to go to school dressed like that then. There's nothing else for it. We'll see what we can sort you out when we get there."

He dropped most of what he was carrying at Parry's feet. "You could at least make yourself useful," he said, "and drag that lot back. I can't believe it. Two crowns!"

Parry followed Gordon back through the narrow streets. The place looked darker and more threatening now as the light faded and the shops shut, but Parry had new hope for his escape. He just had to let Gordon get him back into his own world and then he would use the Stone.

Gordon found the piece of wall he was looking for and Parry thought he saw a flash of silver in Gordon's hand when he tapped on the brickwork. For a moment the wall became a curtain and Gordon, grabbing Parry, stepped through. Once again they were in the sex shop's changing room. Gordon relieved Parry of his cape and hung it with his own on a rail, before leading the way out.

The teenager hung back. About halfway across the shop Parry activated his Stone of Ekoms.

From the street, everything had seemed normal. The shops were closing. There was still a steady stream of late finishers from offices and early theatregoers making their way through the street. The sex shop (which was sometimes there and sometimes not) was present and, for once, it drew attention to itself, billowing out clouds of smoke.

From somewhere inside the smoke Gordon's voice could be heard. "I knew I should have asked you what you bought from the Weasels. I wouldn't mind but that's only a two-bit joke available from any joke store – and when I say 'two-bit' I mean twenty-four pieces. Two *crowns* I gave you. You owe me big time! And the smoke's going to be hell to get out of this suit!"

CHAPTER 3

The morning couldn't come fast enough for Parry.

The evening, however, had lasted forever.

Gordon had insisted on walking to an hotel in order that the air could get some of the smoke out of their clothes. In fact he insisted on walking from the West End to St Pancras, then he set about finding the hotel. He said he remembered a really nice place, but seemed to be some time searching for it. Parry would swear they'd walked up and down the same roads two or three times, and he began to wonder whether it would be one of those mysterious buildings that just appeared in a gap between two others, but no, eventually Gordon found it.

The building had a façade that once must have been very grand, but now was simply tatty and tawdry. When Gordon asked to rent a room the woman behind the counter asked whether that would be for the whole night, or by the hour.

Gordon had to admit the place had gone down a peg or two. He was vague about when he had last visited, leaving Parry to guess it had been a very long time ago.

The evening meal had been a simple affair. The food was lousy, but as Parry was fairly sure that the only rats in the kitchen were the ones eating the scraps, he didn't care too much.

What he did care about was having to share a twin room with Gordon. That worried him. His own firm belief in his irresistibility to gay men meant that he saw the acquisition of a twin room as proof positive of Gordon's interest in him. He slept fitfully, having taken an awfully long time to get to sleep in the first place. Gordon, however, simply spent some time rinsing his clothes, seeing to his beauty regime, then hit the bed and seemingly fell straight to sleep.

The morning, when it arrived, was welcomed by Gordon flinging back the curtains. "Oh what a wonderful…" – dull

London skies greeted him – "well, it's a morning." He turned to look at Parry, who lay on the wall as if it were the floor.

Parry woke when the cold water hit him in the face. The moment he woke the spell was broken and – from lying on the wall – he fell, painfully jamming one arm behind the bedstead.

"Honestly," said Gordon, "I don't know whether it's a greater testament to your increasing magical abilities or your enormously high opinion of yourself. Now rise and shine, you've got a train to catch. And no, I don't think it's broken."

Breakfast was a frustrating affair. Or at least it was for Parry, trying to find a breakfast cereal with enough sugar on it to make it palatable, milk fresh enough to pour, or any part of a cooked breakfast which wasn't purely fat or grease.

For Gordon, however, it was quite a different affair. Whenever Parry looked Gordon seemed to have more to eat. There was salmon (not smoked salmon), there were pancakes, there was muesli with fresh milk and fresh fruit, there was fruit compote, there was yogurt, there were breads and there were rolls, none of which were on the menu at the hotel, and none of which Gordon felt in the least inclined to share.

Settling the bill almost became an event in itself. Gordon commented on how much more expensive things were and then pulled out a bunch of five-pound notes – large white five-pound notes. Parry stared – Gordon demanded "What's wrong now?" before he realized.

Picking up the notes in one hand he apologised to the clerk at the reception desk, and dropping his hand below the desk shook the money. When his hand came back up it was full of contemporary currency. He counted out the cash onto the desk and told the clerk to keep the change. As he and Parry left, the clerk was still examining the notes for authenticity.

If Parry had any hopes that the station from which he would collect the train would be anything special – something wonderful, an encouraging introduction into the magical world – he was sorely mistaken.

Again it took Gordon a little while to decide exactly where he was going. He kept finding landmarks and then pacing the ground out as if he were looking for buried treasure. "Thirty

and the seamy side of magic

paces north, forty paces west, now that wall shouldn't be there," and he would find somewhere else and start again. Where he settled wasn't in St Pancras station itself, or in any of the other local stations at all, but by a bricked-up railway arch in a dirty side street.

"Now," said Gordon, "you'll have to wait here for the train. Should be along in twenty or thirty minutes or so."

Parry glanced up and down the road. There were no train tracks, there wasn't even a magical platform or anyone who could be remotely described as a wizard. A couple who could be very accurately described as drug addicts, but no one you would describe as a wizard.

Piles of cardboard stirred occasionally and shifted, occasionally moved by a rat, more often by a rough sleeper and sometimes by both. Parry did not feel exactly comfortable. He leant on the wall and watched the rubbish being pushed around by the wind. This, he could quite imagine, was the sort of place a body might lay undiscovered for some months. He really didn't feel good.

"I've got some errands to run, a few people to see before I get back to Warthogs. You will wait here and catch the train. You will not wander off. You will leave under no circumstances. If you try and pull one of your famous disappearing acts, smoke screen or no, I will find you and I will kill you. I will do it in the most humiliating way possible. Do you understand?"

Parry nodded. He was beyond believing that he was going to escape from Gordon too easily.

"Good," said Gordon. "Now, no talking to strangers!" With a little wave, Gordon turned and minced off up the road.

Parry watched him stroll into the distance. It was a grey morning but there weren't many other people on the road to hide Gordon in his white suit – and well, it did stand out rather.

Parry was left for some time just leaning against the wall, thinking about all that had happened in less than a day. He had discovered an innate ability to remove female undergarments by willpower alone – he had become a god of underwear. He quickly graduated to blouses and skirts – anything with a fastening. He had briefly held a power over women which he had only ever dreamt of, staff assault alarms excepted. He had been hauled up by the police, followed swiftly by his abduction by possibly the campest person he had ever seen in his life, and now he was probably going to die in a railway arch in a part of London he would never knowingly or voluntarily visit.

The wall behind him shook, then started moving. A couple of trains had already gone past above him, on the track supported by the arch, but this was completely different. He felt he had his back against a moving road. He stood up and turned around. The wall itself was shimmering and seemingly rushing past, like looking at the inside of a tunnel when you are on a moving train, only this time Parry wasn't moving – the wall was.

The closer to the centre of the arch the more pronounced the effect until suddenly the centre of the arch wasn't brick at all. It was now the purple livery of what looked like an old-fashioned railway carriage. Slowly the blurring reduced until the train stopped. Parry heard the sound of the steam engine in the distance and a whistle. The door in front of him swung open. Parry picked up the bag Gordon had given him – a very flowery carpetbag – and, taking a deep breath, stepped into the warmth of the train. The carriage door shut itself behind him.

Parry felt the train start to move, and looked out. St Pancras faded. Suddenly there was brick again and then light. He seemed to be in another more suburban part of London on what appeared to be an ordinary train track.

Parry stood in a narrow corridor that ran the length of the carriage. Facing him on the other side of the corridor were doors to individual compartments which seated six, or perhaps eight smaller kids.

Parry peered in.

There were simply a lot of unfamiliar faces. People were wearing a variety of clothes from traditional wizarding robes to fashionable sports kit. The door at the far end of the carriage opened. For a few moments it got noisier as the interconnecting carriage door allowed in the sound of the track, but Parry was pleased to recognise a face.

and the seamy side of magic 53

"All right, Parry," greeted Freddie. "Thought it must be you. The train doesn't often stop here, not for years! Used to be a station, you know, but that was ages ago."

"Didn't know you would be on the same train," said Parry.

"There's only the one train," said Freddie. "Only the one trip to and one trip back. I saw a carriage with some space in back there," Freddie told him. Parry picked up the carpetbag and followed Freddie Weasel up the carriage and into the next one. Two or three compartments in Freddie slid a door open and stepped inside. Parry followed him. There was indeed some space in the carriage. In fact, only one seat was currently occupied – and by another familiar face – Goodie Deux-Pantoufles.

"Oh it's him," said Parry.

"Him who?" asked Freddie.

"Oh hello! Lovely to see you again. Glad you caught the train. 'spect you're looking forward to starting the new term," said Goodie brightly. Parry ignored him.

"This," said Parry, "is a little creep I ran into when I was buying my uniform. Mr 'Oh didn't you order ahead?' Mr Brown-Nose 'Yes sir, No sir. Mr Money Talks sir'."

Freddie got the idea that some wicked fun might be had. "Right," he said, sitting himself down almost on top of Goodie.

"Hang on," said Goodie. "No need to be like that."

"Oh, no need to be like that," mocked Parry.

"Oh," started Goodie. "I haven't –" but he didn't get the opportunity to finish the sentence. Freddie's elbow clipped him in the face as he made a grab for his bag.

"Oh, isn't this pretty!" Freddie lifted out an ornate magic wand from Goodie's travel bag.

"Give that back," demanded Goodie. "That was my grandfather's!"

"Isn't it pretty," said Freddie. "I do like pretty wands. Shows you're in touch with your feminine side."

"I think Mr Witchy here," said Parry, "has only got a feminine side. He's just a big girl's blouse!"

Freddie began tipping out the contents of Goodie's bag. Clothes started hitting the floor, as did books and occasionally glass equipment which made quite a nasty breaking noise, going from a twenty piece set to a hundred and twenty piece set in a few shattering moments.

Goodie didn't exactly stand by, but one of Freddie's arms was plenty big enough to hold him while he and Parry made derisory comments about his personal items; particularly his pyjamas, slippers with faces on, and a teddy bear.

"I think," decided Parry, "the teddy bear has got to go."

"No!" shouted Goodie.

"You're a big boy now," said Parry. "I think the teddy bear goes out of the window."

This was enough to push Goodie beyond the limit. He lashed out at Freddie, catching him on the side of the face, the blow being painful enough for Freddie to release his grip momentarily.

Goodie went bowling into Parry. A larger lad at that speed would have taken Parry clean off his feet, but instead Parry was able to catch him. Goodie wrestled ineffectually with Parry as Freddie laughed.

Parry was inching his way to the window, holding on to the teddy bear despite Goodie's best efforts. Goodie hit his hand on something hard in Parry's pocket and, still wrestling Parry, he made a grab for a familiar shape. Parry and the teddy bear had practically reached the window when thick choking smoke exploded into the compartment.

It was a couple of minutes before the smoke cleared enough for Freddie and Parry to see, even once the window was down. What they didn't expect to see was Goodie, standing by the door, waiting for them to notice him again.

"Now lads, that wasn't exactly very nice," said Goodie. Parry and Freddie looked at one another. "But I've decided to give you both a second chance," continued Goodie. Parry and Freddie stared at him. "Now I expect it was just high spirits..."

Freddie and Parry bore down on Goodie.

"So I'm sure you'll take this in the same spirit," cried Goodie, at the last instant taking his hands from behind his back and slapping each of the boys with their own wand. Freddie and

Parry flew backwards, slamming against the window end of the compartment.

"That's much more like it boys. Let that be a lesson to you," said Goodie. "Always know where your wand is." He dropped the two wands to the floor and fairly leisurely collected his belongings together again, packing them away into his bags and, wishing the stunned boys a pleasant journey, left the carriage.

Parry and Freddie still hadn't picked themselves up when Hormoany arrived.

"There was this…" Freddie began.

"Gang," offered Parry.

"Yes," agreed Freddie.

"A big gang full of big people," continued Parry.

"Really," said Hormoany, mockingly. "It's just that Goodie Deux-Pantoufles reckons he took the two of you on himself. Gave you what you deserved, he reckons."

"The lying little…" started Parry.

"You wait until we get our hands on him," threatened Freddie, "that little weed. Do you really think he could have touched us?"

"Well," said Hormoany, "he did sound quite convincing. He's even showed us a crystal recording. Still, it's given us all a good laugh!"

Freddie swore under his breath.

༜

Judicita Harmonica, Jude when you wanted something and Hormoany the rest of the time, was a girl who carried about her the obvious evidence of her love of food, but there was nothing particularly unattractive about her, so to Parry she definitely made it into the plain category. The sort of person you wouldn't admit to fancying, but just might get off with at an alcohol-fuelled party – and she could *talk*.

Boy, could this girl talk and – unlike Freddie who quickly settled down to sleep off the wand blast – Parry actually wanted to listen to most of her story, although he wouldn't want to admit it.

She talked about her parents and how they had really wanted her to go to the International Wiccan College, but it was so terribly far away and you had to apply so early and it was unnecessarily expensive, and anyway, exam results weren't the be all and end all of everything.

Hormoany had gone to the Mother Earth Wickham Preparatory School, and was amazed that Parry had had no magical education whatsoever. She really couldn't quite get her head around the idea that someone could be brought up their whole life not using at least a little magic every day. However, to Hormoany and Freddie many of the things that Parry used every day – television, mobile phones, computers – might just as well have been magic.

Hormoany asked if Parry had actually read any of the set books. He just shrugged. Then she asked if he had got the equipment he needed for the term, and he shrugged again. He looked at the embarrassingly brightly decorated carpetbag he had been carrying. Hormoany opened it up and clucked with approval at the various volumes, including one or two which were apparently quite rare background reading books.

Parry was interested to leaf through one particular book. It had examples of a variety of carnivorous plants. How to grow them from seed or cuttings, how to feed them, how best to protect yourself from them, and interesting anecdotes about the more horrific ways people had been consumed by them.

Fatalities at schools of magic, it seemed, could be very high. Hormoany delighted in telling Parry about the various unusual ways students had caused their own deaths – flying broomsticks into solid objects seemed favourite, as did small mistakes in potions.

Even if the mistakes weren't fatal, Parry was assured that the people who had suffered a bad potion often wished they were.

Duels between pupils, once a major cause of death and now technically illegal, weren't really frowned upon. There was something of the old school that felt it toughened the children up – helped prepare them for a place in the world – assuming of course, that it didn't send them into the next.

and the seamy side of magic

And, of course, practical jokes often turned fatal. Freddie boasted that, between them, his brothers had accounted for seven fatalities and a dozen near misses. Although, to be fair, his brothers 'jokes' were often a cover for their gangster style assassination techniques.

The playing fields were another key area of death and injury, particularly the dangerous sport of Kwadwaq, the wizarding game played with broomsticks.

The plants in the school grounds usually took one or two unwary pupils, the plants outside the school grounds a few more. Of course, historically one of the major killers had simply been the school meals. Although that, it had to be said, had improved enormously now that the school had started checking the criminal histories of those working in the kitchens.

The lessons naturally had their own fair share of fatalities. Most were simple accidents, but with a reasonable number being down to the masters.

The school governors had complained somewhat and there had been an altercation in the school grounds, creating a number of interesting new statues.

But all in all the fatalities were kept down to something between ten and fifteen percent of each year's intake. That was considered a reasonable rate of attrition.

Though hungry, Freddie was kind enough to share his sandwich with Parry. Parry took a large bite, but his speed-chewing soon slowed to a stop. Through a full mouth he asked what was in it. Freddie looked at him. "Rat," he said in an 'isn't it obvious' kind of way. Parry spat out his sandwich, coughing and choking.

Hormoany found Parry a drink and then said, "Here, have some of these," offering Parry some crisps. "They're smoky bacon flavour." Parry gratefully stuffed some of the crisps into his mouth, while Hormoany told Freddie off.

"I was only trying to be helpful!" Freddie protested.

"But not everybody likes rat, and what if Parry, who isn't used to the food, got ill?" scolded Hormoany.

Parry, however, had started to wonder what it was he was eating. The crisps he so gratefully had been stuffing into his face were black. He was almost afraid to ask, but he did anyway.

"Well, they're crisped cockroaches of course, smoky bacon flavour," Hormoany told him. "If you are going to be sick, please use the window."

Coughing and spluttering Parry flung himself to the carriage window, pushed the glass down and was violently ill. Hormoany and Freddie were more than happy that he hadn't been sick in the carriage, however, the screams of people further down the train revealed that some people weren't happy at all.

"Wow," enthused Freddy, sticking his own head out of the window, "at least five direct hits!"

By now Parry knew that, wherever this train was going, he would have to escape. The scenery had become less and less familiar as the train travelled. It had started in London on tracks looking pretty much like any others, even passing commuter trains, but as it travelled on it seemed to be taking a route all its own.

Then it was out in the country, and the countryside started looking more and more surreal. Geography, like most academic subjects, wasn't really one of Parry's strong points, but he was fairly certain there were no great blue mountains or large lakes within an hour or two of central London.

The villages that flashed past were more Middle Ages than Middle England, and he seemed to pass a giant ring of standing stones every five minutes or so. Although he had heard of the White Horse or The Giant Man carved into hillsides, the colossal depiction of a copulating couple was not something that had ever featured in any news item he had ever seen.

It was starting to get dark when the train began to buzz with activity. As Parry listened he heard many people moving about. He looked at Freddie and Hormoany.

"We must be getting close now," said Freddie. "Expect we'd better get changed."

'Into what?' Parry asked himself. He had wondered when the fact that he didn't actually own a uniform was going to come up.

and the seamy side of magic

Freddie found it easy to don his uniform. He pulled the flared trousers on under his long kilt, and, taking off his robe, pulled the sweatshirt with the very long flared sleeves over his head.

Hormoany slipped out of the carriage. When she returned she was wearing a smock-like dress in the same rust brown that Freddie was wearing, with a similar stars and moon motif.

The train now began to slow as it entered a weird forest. The trees twisted and turned instead of growing upright, and a strange mist billowed between them.

"The fog is largely for effect," Freddie told Parry. "They do it to impress the first years."

Still, as the sun dropped further, the whole scene seemed less '*A Grand Day Out*' and more a '*Hammer Horror*'.

The carriage jolted as the brakes slammed on, but only Parry nearly lost his seat. Freddie and Hormoany were instinctively braced, for they had known what was coming. The metal on metal screech of the brakes tore through Parry's head.

Freddie lifted his hands to his mouth to shout "For effect!" as the train decelerated. There was a lesser jolt as the brakes were finally released and the train rolled at a walking pace into the station.

The platform was concrete, or perhaps stone, but the buildings – they were certainly wooden buildings – looked as though they had been grown and carved *in situ* rather than built. Up to the first storey all seemed well, but where you might expect a roof there was simply the twisted tangle of boughs and branches which typified the forest they had just travelled through.

It took some time to clamber off the train, and Parry was already being stared at and sniggered about. It might have been the recording that Goodie had made, showing everyone how he had bettered Parry and Freddie, or it might have been the unusual clothes Parry was wearing that attracted the attention; but Parry particularly did not want to bump into those people who clearly had been forced to wash the shoulders of their uniforms and their hair. Those people weren't at all likely to want to be friends.

The brightness of Gordon's white suit had not seemed to diminish in the dusk's half-light. In contrast to the one or two other sombre-robed adult figures Parry could see, Gordon was effusive in his delight.

"Come over here," he was saying to the young arrivals. "Yes, that's right. First years with me. Oh, aren't you looking smart?" he told one eleven-year-old whilst cleaning the kid's face with a licked hanky. "Much better. You've got to look your best."

"Hand in hand," Gordon told his charges. "First years follow me! Hand in hand," he insisted. Some of the young lads clearly thought they were a little too old to be holding another boy's hand, but Gordon just pressed their hands together. It soon became apparent that those Gordon had joined no one was going to tear asunder – at least not without an axe – until Gordon chose to remove the spell.

Parry watched Gordon for a few moments. "What's he up to?" he asked Freddie.

"Oh, he's taking the first years across the lake to the school. I'll say one thing for Gordon, since he's been taking the first years across a lot more of them make it. I think he's been growing some sort of seaweed that attacks the serpents."

A witch was standing at the gate they were approaching. Gordon was clucking over his first years to the right-hand side, and the witch was announcing that the carriages on the left – the horseless carriages – were for sixth-formers only.

The horseless carriages were very much that. Well-presented stage coaches, with everything apart from the horses and coachmen. Not that it seemed to matter much. The carriages seemed to know where they were going, and once the prerequisite number of sixth-form pupils had climbed into each, they set off under their own magical power.

"So," said Parry, "the first years ride across in boats, the sixth form go in these –" he wanted to say cars but he corrected himself – "horseless carriages. So how do we get to the school?"

"We," said Freddie, "walk."

"Across the moat?"

"There's a bridge," Freddie told him.

"And an ogre," said Hormoany. "Just a kitty really!"

As Parry walked along the cobbled road, lit by occasional torches, he could begin to spy the towers of the school through the thinner trees towards the water. In this fading light they looked nightmarish, the towers topped with what seemed to be dishevelled witches hats.

Occasionally something could be seen flittering between the trees, silhouetted against the darkening sky or illuminated by the torches. "Bats?" queried Parry.

"Yeah," said Freddie. "They're great, are bats. I mean, don't you have a postal system yourself? How do you send letters to people?"

"We've got the world wide web," replied Parry.

"Really!" Freddie was amazed. "We don't have spiders *that* big."

"Don't be stupid," said Hormoany. "It's probably lots of little spiders, all working together."

Parry came to a decision. "Could you hold this for me?" he asked, handing his bag to Freddie. Freddie took it reluctantly, looking at Parry and the bag suspiciously.

"Cheers," said Parry, and turned on his heels and ran.

Almost at once Parry realized there were certain things he should have brought with him, had he planned to flee through an enchanted forest.

One, a torch, and two, a sense of direction.

But he did still have his Stone of invisibility, or smoke bomb as he now more correctly thought of it, and he had his wand. The Stone, at least, he knew how to use.

To date, the only thing the wand had achieved had been to knock him sideways twice, and it seemed to be missing a user manual.

And these woods weren't like anything Parry had known.

Parry was following no path, just charging blindly through the thicket which slowed his progress, at times, to less than a crawl. He stumbled upon animal runs, and followed those as far as he could. He tracked along the beds of what must have been streams when the rain came, but at least these muddy paths were largely free of obstruction.

As he moved deeper into the forest fewer plants competed for what little light was able to reach the woodland floor, and so Parry mostly had only the tree trunks to worry about. This was more than enough as he was losing the light, and the half moon in the sky was only able to offer the minimum amount of detail of what was in front of him.

It was about then he ran slam into an upright metal pole, bouncing off onto the ground. Half stunned by the impact, it was a few moments before Parry realized what he had hit.

Bloody stupid place to leave a lamppost, especially if you weren't going to leave the damned thing turned on.

Eyes glowered at Parry from the darkness.

Woodland, in Parry's experience, contained animals, generally small animals. He'd seen foxes and rabbits and squirrels. He was vaguely aware there were probably small rodents too amongst the trees and bushes. He had even seen the body of a badger at the roadside as he was being driven to school, but nothing he could imagine would roar quite the way whatever was out there was roaring, or howl the way something out there was howling.

Or glower, the way something was glowering.

It crossed his mind that once upon a time there had been wolves and bears in Britain's forests. He wondered whether magical people would ever have worried about getting rid of them the way his ancestors had.

Wildlife was all very well in its place, and from Parry's townie perspective, that place was probably Africa. Kenya sounded right, but he wasn't entirely sure.

He *was* sure he could see a couple of eyes. Mean, aggressive, inhuman eyes, low down between the trees. They seemed attached to a snorting nose, and as it moved Parry glimpsed short tusks.

Until now the only wild boars Parry had had to worry about were those blocking his route through the kitchen to the beer at a party. It crossed his mind that boars were supposed to be vegetarian, weren't they?

and the seamy side of magic

But he supposed that here all bets were off. This was a real live animal and so much larger than he had ever imagined. It had to weigh more than him – and now it was charging!

Parry found himself rooted to the spot. That wasn't some metaphorical rooting, but literal – his feet and hands were tangled amongst roots. He was trying to break his way free and the animal was charging. Struggling, he managed to get a degree of movement in his legs but he was still tangled up.

He could only move enough to turn sideways to try and minimise the impact the animal was about to have.

He heard it crashing through the undergrowth and a noise as it hit a bush. Then the animal was squealing. Parry looked up. The boar was caught in a mesh of vine and root. The animal was struggling, but the vine and root simply tightened as it fought.

Then suddenly there came a whip-like crack. At first Parry thought it was the head of a snake launching out and snaring the animal; but as he made out the detail in the near darkness he saw it looked more like a giant Venus flytrap, with tusks where the flytrap would have spikes.

The tusks had speared the boar and it was even now kicking and quivering in its death throes. But already Parry could smell an acidic burning. The roots around his legs loosened. Whatever this was, it was concentrating on its dinner, so Parry did the only reasonable thing possible – he ran.

Parry's flight was painful. It involved bouncing off trees he hadn't seen, torn at by thorns, being tripped and scratched by brambles.

Finally, the trees began thinning out again and he could see a little more clearly in the moonlight. However, he was again slowed because as the trees thinned the bushes thickened, and every step was like wading through barbed wire.

The cries of Parry's imagined wolves and bears were now too distant to be a very real threat to him, and when finally he heard a voice he froze in his tracks.

He caught the sound on breaths of wind. It was faint and had a squeaky quality. It sounded female, and it seemed as though she was calling 'Help me!'

The draw of humanity was too great for Parry to resist. It wasn't as if he had anywhere to run to in particular, he was just running away. Parry followed the noise as best he could, distracted every time he heard a howl or a roar in the distance, or a fluttering in the trees above him.

He'd glance up, and occasionally the moon would be partially obscured by something large and black flying across. He had to keep telling himself it was just the postmen and that they probably weren't vampire bats.

He thought about this.

Okay, maybe it was only fifty-fifty.

As the trees thinned it was a little easier to make out the sound of the voice, always imploring 'Help me! Help me!'

Within the trees the calls bounced around too much, but as he got out of them and into an area of lower bushes he was more able to find the right direction.

He started following a shallow riverbed. A stream flowed in the middle of the channel, but the wide and gently sloping stony banks gave him his best chance to make progress.

Soon he felt sure he must be on top of the cries. He started calling, "Hello, hello. Can you hear me? I'm coming. Where are you?" but the only reply was the repeated 'Help me! Help me!'

He had to walk up and down a little section of bank a couple of times before he was certain he was near as possible to the voice. He climbed up the bank, grabbing branches and boughs to pull himself up, all the time calling out in vain to his maiden in distress.

He couldn't even feel the scratches any more. Whether the adrenaline or the sheer number of injuries had numbed him to the pain, he was driven by the possibility of human contact in what currently seemed a very threatening world.

'Help me! Help me!'

"I'm coming!" called Parry. "Where are you?"

He got closer. He could see the shape outlined on the ground. It looked like a girl lying within the petals of a giant flower. The high cloud passing across the moon made it even

and the seamy side of magic

tougher to see what was happening, but even in Parry's adrenaline-fuelled state, something seemed wrong.

The wind blew; the great petals folded across. 'Help,' cried the voice. The wind weakened and the petals relaxed. 'Me!' called the voice.

Again the wind gusted, the petals compressed. 'Help.' The petals relaxed as the wind died. 'Me!' came the voice.

Parry realized what was wrong with the sound.

It had a reedy quality, as if it were an instrument and not a human voice. A reedy siren's call. The cloud across the moon cleared for a few moments. Parry could see clearly how this nightmare plant had shaped within itself a rough facsimile of a human. The lure lay in the centre of the plant, between green gaping tusked jaws.

Almost too late Parry remembered his feet. He started hauling them out of the roots that were trying to bind him, pushing into his shoes, finding their way up his trouser leg.

Parry vaguely remembered a horror movie he had once seen. The fear that these plants might rip his clothes off and probe him in places he hadn't convinced fauna to probe, let alone flora, scared him even more than the memory of what had just happened to the wild boar.

Tearing himself from the grasping roots and acting on no more than the instinct for survival, he threw himself back towards the riverbed.

The roots kept his shoes as souvenirs, but Parry was beyond caring. He stumbled and slid as he reached the shallow riverbed. The stones were largely rounded by the water, but his feet were already torn.

Parry could only imagine what other horrors lay in this parallel world into which he had been dragged. He shook, physically and mentally exhausted. Perhaps this riverbed was where he was going to curl up and die. He shrank to his knees, but something caught his eye through the trees on the other side of the stream.

He wasn't sure if he had really seen it, so he painfully stood back up, moving his head to try and catch sight again of what he thought he had seen, but no, there it was – definitely a light. There was a light on the other side of the stream!

Suddenly Parry was alive again. Awake and focused, aware only of the cold night air on his face and the need to reach the light – civilisation – safety.

He began back along the riverbed, past where he had joined it, and onward toward the light.

The stream he was following soon joined a much wider watercourse. It became a small river of dark, slow-moving water, hiding heaven knows what underneath.

There had to be a way across the water. There just had to. He couldn't see a light like this just to find no way to reach it. He couldn't believe that even *his* luck could be that bad.

Parry was forced to hug the bank of the river for some time, painfully aware he had passed the light on the other bank and was now getting further away from it with every step. But he couldn't cross the stream or the river, so he had only one direction in which to go.

Finally Parry got his first break – there was a bridge up ahead.

It was still a fair distance away, but it was in sight and that was all that mattered. He scrambled along the soft banks. Sometimes the muddy earth fell away from him, and sometimes it was secured by willow roots and the other trees along the riverbank, but he made steady progress. There was a bridge, and he had to get to it.

For brief moments he had to wade in the river, but his brushes with eels – or perhaps the tails of serpents – made sure he got out of the water as soon as humanly possible.

At last, Parry reached the bridge. It was made of stone, having three arches spanning the width of the river.

A cobbled pathway led back into the forest through which Parry had fled; across the bridge the path widened into what looked like a tamer, more civilised road.

Pleased to have something solid underfoot, Parry trotted across. But the night had by no means finished with him yet.

Something long and thick reached out across the road in front of him. Parry froze. He could imagine another of those plants reaching up from the river to grab him. Then another limb reached up over the edge of the bridge, and Parry realized that at least this was animal rather than vegetable.

A torso drew itself over the wall of the bridge, and finally an enormous creature stood in the middle of the road, blocking Parry's path across the bridge.

"Oh, bugger!"

"Well, 'good evening' is more customary," said the creature in a low rasping growl. "Manners cost nothing, you know."

"I, I..." began Parry.

"Were you planning to cross the bridge?" it asked.

"I was trying to make it to the house. You see the house? That's where I'm going."

The creature turned its big head over one shoulder and then looked back at Parry. "You wear no robe I recognise," it said. "An insignia, that is strange also. Are you far from home, young man?"

"You could say that," answered Parry.

The creature smiled, as if to say 'good'. It looked at the state of Parry. "And I'm guessing you travel alone, no? Experiencing difficulty, yes? Seeking help?"

"You could say that," repeated Parry.

"Oh good! So very good. It's so rare I come across an undefended traveller these days. A troll could starve to death with so many uniforms tramping across, be they officers, or wizards, or apprentices. Not allowed to touch them, I'm not. But strangers, ah, is bread and butter is strangers. Or meat and drink, to be more precise, yes?"

"I only want to..." began Parry.

"You have purpose in life now, child. Probably a greater purpose than you have ever served before. You will feed and sustain me," said the troll as it moved nearer. "Part of the great web of life. I, you understand, am at the top of the food chain, whereas you..."

Parry stepped backwards, stuttering incoherently as words failed him.

"Now don't be upset," said the troll. "I'm a civilised creature. Honestly. I'll make sure you feel nothing. After a short while, anyway."

Parry needed a weapon. Even with what remained of his adrenaline pumping through him as hard as ever it could, his body was stiff and sore. He couldn't run far, and didn't think that even at his fittest he could outrun such a large being with such unusually long limbs.

Parry had to think. Think. He patted down his pockets.

"I've got money," he said, holding out the Weasel brothers' counters.

"Yes, yes," said the troll.

Parry found the Stone in his pocket. "I have the Stone of Ekmos," he said.

"What," asked the troll, "would I do with another stone?"

"But, but..." began Parry.

"Very well," said the troll, "I'll examine your belongings once I've eaten you. I really am quite peckish."

Then Parry's hand felt the wand. Really, some form of machine gun would have been more useful, but the wand would have to do.

"Stand back!" he cried, flourishing the wand and pointing it at the creature.

"Stand back or you'll what?" asked the troll. "You'll poke me with your little stick?"

"Wand!" screamed Parry, "it's my wand, and I am a wizard! Cross me and you shall forever regret it!"

The troll considered this for a few moments. It studied Parry's general appearance, the missing shoes, the torn clothing, the lacerations.

"No, I really don't believe that I shall regret it. I think I am going to have to take my chances, yes?" it said, calling Parry's bluff. "There's a good dinner."

The troll advanced.

Parry shook the wand at it.

"Kill! Maim! Disfigure!" Parry shouted, but to no avail.

Fear took hold as the creature was nearly upon him.

Parry screamed. "No!"

The troll jolted.

"No, no, no!" repeated Parry, channelling his fear through the wand. The troll jolted and jolted and jolted, but even channelled by the wand, Parry's magic was doing no more than slowing the creature's advance.

"No!" Parry screamed, and suddenly the creature's clothing seemed to fall apart. The great leathery trousers on the troll fell, tripping the creature. Its coat loosened and wrapped around its body as it fell.

Parry ran. He leapt up onto the wall at the side of the bridge and ran as fast as he could. The troll had landed heavily and was trying to shake its arms and legs loose from the uncontrolled clothing. As soon as he was past the troll Parry leapt down onto the road, nearly falling as he did so, and with every scrap of his remaining strength he ran and he ran.

The troll sat itself up, grumbling.

"Is that any way to behave, is it? Give them a wand and they all think they're Merlin!"

CHAPTER 4

In the darkness he almost missed it, but leading from the relatively wide roadway Parry had been following was a smaller path toward the house and the light he had seen. The neatly arranged gardens couldn't have seemed further from the chaos of the woodlands he had left. The only scary shadows were those cast by bushes trained into amusing shapes – cats, birds and the like.

Parry unlatched the metal gate set in neatly trimmed hedging, and followed the garden path. Here patches of cosily arranged flowers gently sighed in their beds, almost as if generating a breeze of their own in this sheltered spot.

A couple of gnomes were fishing in the garden pond, and Parry didn't even notice them staring at him. They soon lost interest in him when distracted by a fish taking their bait.

He could hear a tinkling of what sounded like sleigh bells as he approached the door. He soon realized the ringing was the sound of the plants hanging in baskets by the porch, although – like the sighing of the flowers in the garden – he wasn't sure that there was really enough wind about for the plants to be making all that noise.

Parry hadn't thought about what he was going to say. 'Help! I've been attacked! I've been abducted! I need to get back to London'? But he was relieved to be approaching the large house. The brick and slate construction felt familiar. At least, he thought, it wasn't gingerbread. The house looked like a sprawling old rectory. He knocked on the door.

A sound of splashing caught his attention for a moment. He looked back towards the pond. The two gnomes were pleased with themselves for having landed a carp. Suddenly the door opened. Parry turned, and was almost blinded by what seemed like very bright lights to his moonlight accustomed eyes.

and the seamy side of magic

"Oh there you are! Got a little lost, did we? We were getting *so* worried. Took a wrong turn, hmm? Just look at the state of you. We must get you inside and cleaned up. Wouldn't want you to miss the sorting, now would we?"

Gordon ushered the dumbfounded boy inside and closed the door.

༺♥༻

The walk to the main building felt like it took forever. The old pair of Gordon's gardening slippers didn't make it any more comfortable, and nor did the fact that for the first ten minutes Gordon was fussing around by his goldfish pond trying to mend the wire mesh the gnomes had cut.

"I wouldn't mind so much if they were at least eating their catch," Gordon complained, "but the little poachers only ever fish for sport. It's just the shiny colours that attracted them. Trophy hunters the lot of them."

Parry, who was learning a healthy respect for the local flora and fauna, stayed close to Gordon as they marched back up along the road to the huge school building. Warnings like 'mind the carnivoregilea' and 'don't tread on the needlegrass because we'd be forever getting the blood out of my slippers' kept Parry pretty solidly in the middle of the road, just a few steps behind Gordon.

The school was approached through wrought-iron gates set in a tall wall. Ominously, ghoulish figures sat upon both of the gates' pillars, as if to scare away unwelcome intruders. '*Warthog Approved School of Magic and Wizardry*' proclaimed the rusty metal sign arching over the entrance.

"You know," Gordon told him, "they've only just cut the 'k' out of 'magick' and they're already arguing to add the word 'Wicca'. Some people have no sense of tradition. Come along!"

Now Parry could see the belfries and the towers and the spires of the school. Yellow and orange lights illuminated the windows, and the towers appeared shadowy, even misshapen. Even up close like this, some of the towers appeared to be wearing wizarding hats of their own, crumpled on top of their long brick and stone necks.

"Normally, of course," said Gordon, "you'll be using the students' entrances around the side and the back, but as it's your first day you can come in through the 'grand' entrance."

And grand it was.

Two huge arching doors, fit for giants, stood at the top of a long and wide flight of stone steps. The flagstones were worn by many generations of feet, or occasionally, by the same feet through a single very long generation.

"We'll use the wicket," called Gordon brightly, leading Parry through a small hatch set in the base of the left-hand door. Parry had to crouch to get through without bumping his head, but what he saw on the other side was quite amazing. It was almost like being in a cathedral; perhaps a cathedral crossed with a country manor house.

Atop tall stone pillars were great wooden beams and stone arches supporting the vaulted ceiling. A grand staircase swept down from the gallery above, its scale emphasizing the sheer size of the structure that contained it. The atmosphere itself seemed infused with the smell of stone and wood and open fires, of a million school meals and tens of thousands of bottles of sherry. The Great Lobby, large as it was, was cluttered with students, many calling to one another. Others, the younger ones, gawping at the building much as Parry had.

The brown uniforms were very much in evidence, and amongst the students passed sombre robed witches and wizards. Some of the tutors were happy to acknowledge familiar faces, pleased to see the return of their young charges. Others batted students out of their path with deft blows to their ears or shins, as they made their way through to the Great Hall via the grand doors set in the left-hand wall.

"Oh, we'll just have to do," said Gordon, slapping Parry's jacket a few times in some effort to tidy it up. "We'll see about you later. You join this queue," placing Parry in the centre of the room. "You'll all be called. You just file in then. Follow everyone else – you'll be fine."

and the seamy side of magic

'Queue?' thought Parry. He looked around, and saw nothing resembling a queue in the crowd, until he looked down. He was at the back of a loosely-formed queue of what he guessed were ten or eleven-year-olds, leading up to the great door where a witch was ensuring – from scrolls and scrolls of paper – that she had the right number of new students, the right names, and that they were arranged in the right order. She fussed her way along the line, swapping pupils to and fro until she finally reached Parry.

Her gaze moved from the head of the last child to stare at Parry's jacket pocket. Then her head came up, to see Parry head and shoulders taller than she was herself. She flicked through the papers, and then found the scribbled note. "You must be Hotter, yes?" Parry nodded. She took him by the arm, and led him down the queue.

"Kabana, Jasmine, Huntington, Holt, yes, Hotter – this is your place. Yes." She seemed quite pleased with herself. And, after inserting Parry between two students who had quite clearly been in the middle of a conversation, she returned to the head of the queue.

"Excellent," the witch announced, "we're all here, and, oh, it sounds like they're ready for us."

From behind the great doors, a deep, chiming gong sounded out; once, twice, thrice. The great doors opened to reveal a hall. Well, the Great Lobby was huge: this hall was simply gigantic. Perhaps the young students around him had known what to expect, but Parry himself was stunned at the enormity of it. Huge tables stretched away into the distance, with long lines of students sitting at them. In the distance was a platform holding a table full of witches and wizards, the wizard in the centre sitting on an almost throne-like seat.

Parry stepped across the threshold into the Great Hall. To his horror, the distant walls appeared to rush toward him as the hall seemed to rapidly shrink. Parry almost lost his footing, and was grateful for the hands that caught him. A witch and a wizard were just the other side of the doors, steadying people as they filed through.

"False perspective doorway," said the elderly but kindly seeming witch. "For effect you know. Always catches them the first time."

The hall was now simply a large hall, not the unfeasible size it had seemed when looking in from outside, but still a very respectable size. Just what you might expect in any big boarding school or university. But something else had caught Parry's attention.

As he had stumbled, he had looked skyward, and seen – where he expected a ceiling – a vast canopy of stars. It was as if he were looking straight up into the night sky itself. The wizard on the door followed Parry's gaze and glanced up himself.

"Damnation!" exclaimed the wizard. "They were supposed to have that fixed during the holidays! Can't get a decent roofer for charm nor money these days. Now I suppose we'll have to put up with building work until the solstice break!"

Parry followed the line of young students down the centre aisle of the hall. To each side of him were long tables full of students from second to upper sixth years. Each of the tables was hung with one of four flags, all four of which were also displayed behind the wizards' head table. The line of first years and Parry came to a halt. The din of conversation from the tables quietened to nothing. Everyone looked expectantly towards the powerfully built wizard with the long grey-flecked beard who sat on the great throne at the centre of the top table.

Oblivious to this, the Headmaster kept eating.

The school waited patiently.

The Headmaster started on another joint of meat.

The witch to the Headmaster's left tugged on his sleeve. He glanced at her and, taking a chunk of meat from his plate, dropped it onto hers. She tugged his sleeve again for a few moments to regain his attention, and shaking her head beckoned him closer. She whispered something in his ear. The Headmaster looked up and stared for a moment, as if it were the first time he had seen the queue of students standing in the main aisle. Then he stared for a few moments at the empty seat to his right, and then looked around the hall.

and the seamy side of magic

He saw the man he was looking for. Following his gaze Parry saw what looked like a senior student carrying a chair, and behind him an older wizard – missing his wizard's hat – wearing crisp pinstriped robes. He had over his outstretched arms a long garment of off-white cloth. He was standing patiently, staring towards the Headmaster. With a wave of a bone, the Headmaster beckoned them forward.

With all due procession, the two marched to the space in front of the top table and the student placed the chair on the floor. Excused, the chair-bearer returned to his seat amongst the long tables. The hatless wizard unfurled the item he was carrying and held it above his head so that everyone could see the grey long johns. He showed each of the tables in turn, then cried: "Behold! Behold, the long johns of power, bequeathed to us by our founders. The only item to have survived the fiercely-contested change of academic management."

The Headmaster, wiping the better part of a leg of lamb from his beard, gestured towards the underwear, and the long johns seemed to fill with a life of their own. They stood up on the chair, turned and leant backwards a little. The flap in their seat began to open and close like a mouth as the long johns spoke:

I was woven from yak hair, asbestos and magic
And worn by mages with powers fantastic
For hundreds of years I'd support the behind
Of mystical men and those of their kind

Down through the ages I've discreetly absorbed
Wizards' waste magic and wisdoms abroad
I've never been washed and am proudly unchaste
As I devour the power from wizardly waste

The selection is easy, an unworrying feat
So take a deep breath, and attend to my seat
From three of these houses you'll forever be barred
The Archer, The Canute, The Midas, The Sade

The Archers are idle, slippery, conniving
When the going gets tough, they're always found skiving

*Their strength is deception, at fraud they're the best
After one hour's work they demand six hours rest!*

*The Canutes have a feeling of shameless self-worth
You'll find yourself wishing they'd been smothered at birth
But treachery and treason amongst them you'll find
You'd better beware an approach from behind*

*The Midas have money and will always want more
At alchemy they try, but they've tried that before
If, in the end, nothing touched turns to gold
They'll resort to plan 'B' and steal from the old*

*The Sades are the oldest and wisest by far
But their methods of torture are deemed quite bizarre
You'd better not cross them, you'll be made to repent
Fluffy handcuffs and whips a favourite torment*

*I shall select you, by virtue of great wit
Into the house where your defects best fit
If, in my decision, fault you do find
Ask yourself carefully, who speaks from behind?*

Introductions complete, the immaculately dressed wizard who had brought forth the long johns consulted a parchment and called the first name on the list. The boy at the head of the queue ran forward and, grabbing the long johns, pulled them on. Almost at once, as if by an unseen force, he was twisted around and bent slightly forward. The flap at the back of the long johns loudly announced "Archer House!"

One of the tables to Parry's extreme right burst into raucous applause, yelling and whooping, and after a couple of false starts settled into a chant. "Archer, cha cha cha! Archer, cha cha cha!" – stamping their feet and bashing the table with their hands. Among the revellers, Parry spotted Goodie Deux-Pantoufles.

The next child, a girl, came forward. She pulled the long johns up under her skirt, and was immediately flipped around. The skirt lifted as the long johns pronounced "Midas House!"

and the seamy side of magic 77

She whipped off the underwear and joined a considerably less raucous table to Parry's left.

The next child, another girl, ran forward. She was flipped around, the long johns announcing "Sade House!"

The table on the extreme left of the hall burst into life. "What do we want?" the chant went up. "Kinky girls! – When do we want them? – Now!"

The next two students were received by the Midas and Canute tables, with some semblance of order. Then the Archer table received its second recruit, and burst again into chant. "Archer, cha cha cha! Archer, cha cha cha!"

Then it was Parry's turn.

Conscious of being so much older than the other students he almost jogged over to the chair, sat down and pulled the long johns over his trousers. Immediately the strangest sensation came over him, as if he had lost control over his body from the waist down. Only his head and his arms seemed to belong to him any more as he was turned around, bracing himself against the back of the chair to save toppling over.

The long johns felt as if they were stuffed with a hundred pairs of hands, squeezing and probing every little piece of his flesh from his calves to his waist.

'Mm, interesting, interesting,' said a voice in Parry's head. 'Older than most of our students, this one has been lost to us for a time.' 'This one has the worldliness of an Archer,' said another voice. 'Pride of a Canute,' said another. 'Greed would make a Midas of this child,' said the first voice.

Parry's head jolted up, his eyes wide, as his most intimate areas were firmly squeezed. 'Filthy little boy!' cried a fourth voice in his head. 'Lustful,' said the first voice, 'we like that.' 'Filthy,' said the second voice. 'Perverted,' said the third.

Parry felt a sudden release of the pressure as the flap on his bottom opened. A voice sang out to the whole hall, "Sade House!"

Feeling as though he had control of his body again Parry whipped the long johns off as quickly as he could, and slung them down on the chair. The table to the far left of the hall had already burst into chant – "What do we want? – Dirty perverts!

– When do we want them? – Now! What do we want? – Dirty perverts! – When do we want them? – Now!"

Parry crossed the hall to join his new school house. He started to walk toward the bottom end of the table, as he had seen the other newcomers do, but a hand grabbed him as he went past. It was Freddie.

"All right, my son!" congratulated Freddie, "Good on you!" He slapped Parry's back. "Sit down here with me." Hormoany, sitting opposite, was smiling at him as Parry took his seat.

"Knew you were a dirty bugger," said Freddie, "the minute I set eyes on you. Welcome to 'Perv Central'."

Parry looked up and down the table. He recognized Freddie's brothers amongst the older pupils towards the top end of the hall.

"Didn't think you were going to make it when you legged it into the woods," said Freddie. "Thought that was the last I'd ever see of you."

"Those woods are cursed. You do know that?" asked Hormoany, a genuine concern in her voice.

"No," Parry told them emphatically. "I certainly did not know that. Why didn't you stop me?"

Hormoany stared at her empty plate on the table. Freddie shrugged. "It's not like you owe me money or nothin'," he explained.

The questioning was cut short as the table erupted once more; the long johns had again found an individual twisted enough to join Sade House.

"Have you been up to the dorms yet?" Hormoany asked.

"No," replied Parry. "I've literally only just got here, lined up and been sorted."

"Well, I suppose you can bunk with me," said Freddie. "I've been keeping the extra bunk in my room free, out of respect."

"Out of respect for me?" asked Parry, touched.

"No," said Freddie. "Out of respect for my personal space, but it's the least I can do, considering. A guy without a place to bunk can have real problems in this part of the world."

Parry wasn't sure what Freddie was driving at, on the basis that he was fairly certain that the school had bunks for everybody. Then again, they might have been relying on the odd troll and a few serpents to thin the numbers out a little.

"Did you put my stuff in your room?" Parry asked.

Hormoany stared pointedly at Freddie. Freddie considered his answer. "Well," he said, "your stuff is in the dorms, certainly."

"In *our* dorm?" Parry asked again.

"Largely," said Freddie. "The thing to concentrate on," he told Parry, "is that you've got a bunk. You'd be in real trouble without a bunk."

Parry was getting a little suspicious. "Is the stuff in *our* room, Freddie?"

"The carpetbag is in our room, yes," said Freddie.

"And the stuff in it?" asked Parry.

"Well, it's like this, you see. It was a long way to carry a bag, and you were missing, presumed consumed, or at least composting. It was a long way to carry a dead man's bag. There were expenses to consider, shoe-leather and disbursements."

"Disbursements?" asked Parry.

"Well, my brothers nicked some stuff, but I got a good price on what I had left. Should be able to trade some of it back."

"A good price? You mean you sold my stuff?"

"Well, not for money as such," Freddie explained. "There are some intangible assets to consider."

"Such as?" asked Parry.

"Future contracts, options, dungeon time…"

"Dates," Hormoany clarified.

"We can double-date. Some of them –" Freddie leant forward encouragingly – "are human!"

Once the noise from another new Sade addition calmed down, Hormoany changed the subject. "So, how did you get here? Did they send wizards to hunt you down?"

"That Gordon," considered Freddie, "can be a difficult man to get away from."

"Did they send dogs?" asked Hormoany, clearly enthralled by the subject. "Did they send packs of hounds to hunt you down, Parry?"

'No. I ran in a big circle, nearly got myself killed a couple of times, and then I knocked on Gordon's door,' Parry thought.

"Yeah," said Parry. "Wizards with dogs, monstrous dogs. I'd have got away from them, too, if I hadn't had to fight off the troll. Slowed me down, that troll did."

Hormoany was wide-eyed. "You fought a troll?"

Freddie was more thoughtful. "The only troll round here that I know of is just out these gates here, under the bridge."

"No," insisted Parry. "This was miles away. Miles and miles. You should have seen the monsters in the forest, and the killer plants."

"You sure you've had no wizarding training?" Freddie asked, giving him a sideways look.

"No, none," said Parry.

"Not even a bit of witching on the side?" asked Freddie. "Or a protection charm? Anti-monster curse?"

"No. Guess I'm just a natural."

"You're amazing," said Hormoany, not quite getting up the nerve to play footsie with him yet.

"Granted, you certainly beat the odds," said Freddie thoughtfully, still giving him the odd sideways look, as if he believed that he might have been dabbling in a bit of that girlie witchcraft after all.

Finally, with students Xavier and Yüan going to the Midas and Canute houses respectively, the sorting was over. All the tables clapped and cheered as the long johns were folded ceremoniously and carried off by the wizard with the pinstripe robes (the Bursar, as Hormoany informed Parry).

The Bursar returned, sounded a gong, and imperiously declared "May the feasting begin," seemingly oblivious to the fact that Bol d'Areth had been eating since before anyone else had entered the hall, and showed no signs of slowing down now.

Parry's side plate shook for a moment, and suddenly there was a biscuit on it. The tables themselves trembled; the large tureens – placed roughly every six students – vibrated, then were suddenly filled with all manner of food: meats and stews and vegetables.

and the seamy side of magic

Freddie started heartily tucking in to the contents of the nearest tureen. Parry was starving, but still looked at the contents suspiciously.

"What's in it?" he asked Freddie. Freddie paused for a moment to consider his answer. Parry was learning that this was generally not a good sign.

"Do you want me to say 'rat'?" Freddie asked.

"No," said Parry. "I really don't want you to say 'rat'."

Freddie considered for a further moment, his ladle in mid-air. "Nothing," he said, "nothing's in it." And ladled an ever more generous amount into his own bowl.

"Here, have some bread," offered Hormoany, passing Parry a couple of black slices, and managing to kick him with the heel of her shoe, just inside his knee.

"Ow," winced Parry. "Wotcha do that for?"

Hormoany, embarrassed, mumbled her apology whilst looking the other way. 'Always remember,' she scolded herself, 'take shoes off before playing footsie.'

Parry eyed the black bread suspiciously. He guessed it must be pumpernickel or something so – his hunger getting the better of his reservations – he bit into it, chewed once, chewed twice. He looked at Hormoany and through his mouthful of food asked, "What kind of bread is this?"

Hormoany was doing her best to avoid him over the whole kicking incident, but Freddie answered for her.

"Insect bread," said Freddie. "Do you have that at home?"

Parry couldn't spit out the contents of his mouth fast enough. He grabbed a jug from the table. Pointing at it, he asked Freddie, "Water?"

"Yeah, water," Freddie confirmed. Parry started swigging the water, spitting the first couple of mouthfuls out on the floor on the side away from Freddie. This caused obvious irritation to his neighbour on that side of him, encouraging her to budge away as far as the crowded table allowed.

"Water of what, I dunno," mumbled Freddie, thankfully too quietly for Parry to hear.

Parry reached for the biscuit on his side plate, this being the only thing he was relatively sure of on the table.

"No," hissed Hormoany. "You can't have that until after. They're *very* strict."

Reluctantly, Parry put the biscuit back. Looking at the high table, raised on a small stage area, he reluctantly concluded that those witches and wizards could most probably be very strict indeed.

Parry whiled away the rest of the course wondering what interesting diseases he could catch from the rats and bugs which seemed to be the mainstay of this alien diet. Finally the gong sounded again, the gong the Bursar had struck to start the feast, and the dinner plates and the bowls emptied. Once the vibration had finished it was hard to believe there'd ever been food on them at all.

Then the gong was sounded again, and the bowls and the jugs vibrated once more. This time they were filled with desserts. Here Parry saw an opportunity not to starve. Most of the other students were avoiding the fruit bowls, and there were at least some fruits in there that Parry recognized. While everyone else was helping themselves to various versions of sweet mushy stuff, Parry grabbed a handful of bananas, and after carefully inspecting them to ensure they held no nasty surprises, wolfed them down.

He eyed the contents of other people's plates. Apart from what was obviously some sort of candied cricket and something else that looked like jellied worms, the cakes, the trifles, the sponges, the custards and the biscuits on the table seemed largely edible. He decided not to risk asking what anything was. If it tasted all right, and most stuff did, he was going to eat it and try not to think about it.

He was just going to have to do his best to survive on desserts. By the time the Bursar rang the gong again and the food began to disappear from the tables, even Parry was feeling a bit stuffed.

"May I have your attention, please?" asked the Bursar, in the manner of a man expecting one's full attention, please or no please. "Our esteemed Headmaster, the venerable Bol d'Areth, would like to say a few words."

and the seamy side of magic

The Bursar led the top table in some polite clapping. The purpose of this seemed to be to attract Bol d'Areth's attention away from the mountainous cake he was busily demolishing. He looked up and down the table and decided it was time to brush the crumbs and cake slices from his beard and stand to say the expected few words, however much he disliked the chore.

"Delighted to see you all, of course. So many of you have survived to rejoin us, and so many fresh lambs to the, to the first year. I seem to remember that your survival rate will be somewhat higher than average. Or possibly that's next year. Either way will be pretty good. Above all please remember, whatever the petty squabbles or issues of the day, however large or small, *leave me out of it*."

The venerable Bol d'Areth, the unpleasant duty done, retuned to his demolition of a fruitcake.

The Bursar stood and led a little polite clapping.

"With your indulgence Headmaster, I also have a few words to say. Remember, no running in the corridors, and no skulking in the corridors after midnight. The caretaker, Mr Grimshaw, detained five pupils last year for such offences. If we have no more instances this year, he assures us he will return them in time to rejoin next year's classes. Note too that all Kwadwaq fixtures will be played on the new pitch, in respect of the memory of last year's team.

"Also be aware that, in common with the other major wizarding schools, we are this year abandoning the apothecaries' weights in favour of the avoirdupois system. Please ensure all your measuring instruments are to the new scale, and purchased from *reputable* certified sources."

"Is he looking at me?" asked Hannibal Weasel.

"I think he's looking at me," said his brother Damian.

"During this week we shall be hosting a delegation from Ogs-Warth School of Witchcraft to discuss closer academic ties. The Headmaster will of course be expecting every courtesy to be shown during the visit.

"Owing to the number of avoidable casualties," the Bursar continued, "there will be only one token fagging session this term. If you would care to open your fortune cookies; forth-

formers serving lower sixth and fifth-formers serving upper sixth."

As if on cue, the many hands of the fourth and fifth forms reached for their large biscuits, cracking them open to find the tubes of paper inside, and stuffing the biscuits into their mouths.

Parry regarded his with fresh suspicion. "What's this fagging?" he asked Freddie.

"Oh," said Freddie, spraying biscuit crumbs across the table, "it's where you're supposed to show respect for your senior students by basically being their slave. Used to be it would go on all year.

"But the..." he furrowed his brow as he tried to remember the school notice – 'rate of attrition was deemed unacceptable'."

Freddie unfurled his piece of paper, and read the name. "Farquar Jensen. Bats-teeth, I'll be ironing underpants all night."

Freddie caught Parry's worried expression.

"Oh, you'll be all right. It's just a bit of an irritation, mainly. Long as you don't get Vlad the Impaler, they're fine these days."

"Vladimir Choucesco?" asked Parry.

"Yeah. How did you know?" wondered Freddie, choking as he caught sight of the name on Parry's piece of paper. "Ah," he said, then after a short pause, "well, on the plus side it looks as though I'll have my room to myself again."

Freddie's brothers were making their way down the table, snatching the pieces of parchment off each of the fifth years and checking the name before moving along. Freddie caught their eye and nodded his head towards Parry.

"What?" demanded Parry.

"Sorry mate," Freddie shook his head sadly. "You did so well in the forest and everything."

The Weasel twins arrived at each of Parry's shoulders and laid heavy hands upon him. "Wotcha doing?" he asked. "Gerroff!"

"We're here to escort you to Mr Choucesco," announced Hannibal.

"He has a certain reputation, you see," explained Damian.

and the seamy side of magic 85

"Precedes him, it does," said Hannibal.

"And Mr Choucesco likes to ensure his fags get to him in one piece. How many pieces they leave in is their own business."

"Pays well, he does," said Damian.

Hormoany seemed tearful as Parry was lifted by the shoulders from the table. Freddie shook him by the hand. "It's been good knowing you," he said, relieving an oblivious Parry of his watch. "See you around, then, eh?"

※

Gordon's advance down the corridor wasn't as purposeful as it might have been. A few good solid strides, followed by the distraction of an urn that needed straightening or a surface that needed dusting. Now and again, the wooden twig he was holding in his hand would turn and poke him, and he would say, "Yes, yes, just a minute," and follow the divining rod's insistent pointing.

He would sometimes come across an open doorway. He liked to lean in and pass some comment before closing the door: "Enjoy that now. You won't be able to do that when you're older"…"Interesting use of a trapeze"…"How very Kama Sutra of you."

Finally, at the divining rod's insistence, Gordon knocked on a door. "Well, it would be this one, wouldn't it?" he said to himself. The door opened a crack.

"No thank you," said an accent that contrived to be both east European and terribly upper class. "We have no gardening needing doing, thank you." The door tried to shut. The divining rod intervened, and then the door was flung open and the doorkeeper went tumbling back across the room.

"Very witty, I'm sure," Gordon glanced around the well-appointed apartment. "Now, let me see. Ah, there you are Parry."

"This is *my* session," protested Vladimir angrily, snatching up a hot poker from the fire and waving it in Gordon's face. "You can't come in here just like that!"

Gordon took the proffered poker by its heated end, relieving it of the crumpet skewered upon it. He took a nibble. "Overdone," he opinioned.

Gordon handed the poker back to Vladimir. There was a sizzling sound before the poker was dropped to the floor.

"Oh dear, oh dear, oh dear," Gordon said, looking at Parry tied across an exercise horse. "Same old tricks, eh Vlad?"

Gordon released the ropes with the merest gesture of his hand.

"Official school business, I'm afraid. The Headmaster needs to see this one, and anyway, I can't let you do that to him. Or at least, not while he still owes me money. Come on, Parry. Don't want to keep the Headmaster waiting. Pull your trousers up, there's a good lad.

"Ooh," Gordon said, spotting the blistering on Vladimir's hand. "I should get that looked at if I were you. Mr Tollopoff might have a poultice for it, or a really good healing manure, I daresay."

"He was going to – going to…" blubbed Parry.

"Now don't worry," Gordon calmed him. "I know, I know. But I'm sure something nasty will get you in the end." Gordon steered Parry out of Vlad's room and up the hallway.

"Where are we going? Why does the Headmaster want to see me?"

"We are going to find out who your parents are, Parry."

"Really?" asked Parry. "You can do that for me?"

"For you be buggered," replied Gordon. "You don't think the finest education comes for free do you? We need to find out who to bill."

ை

Bol d'Areth stared from the window of his office. He sat in a huge leather chair which, though aged, had never quite gotten around to wearing out. Like the rest of the furniture in the room – the great table, the heavy desks – it was substantial, substantial in a way that you felt its presence even before you'd entered the room.

and the seamy side of magic

The Headmaster gazed out over the four great trees. The birch tree in the quadrant, the yew on the other side, the elm further along, and the golden willow by the lake. He remembered planting each of them.

Hell of a day, that was.

And then he had chosen where his office was to be, where he could see the trees. Actually building the new floor had been someone else's problem.

There was a knock on his door. The Bursar peered in. "Gordon is here, sir," he said. "He's brought the boy with him."

The Bursar barely acknowledged Gordon and Parry as he returned to his desk. He busied himself with his preparations. A large pewter bowl with runes inscribed around its broad rim sat on his desk. It was full of water, to which he had been carefully adding charmed sands, potions and other magical ingredients, whilst mumbling the necessary incantations under his breath.

The water shimmered, and became a dull bluish-grey colour, much like that of the pewter itself.

Gordon busied himself, clipping at a bonsai tree and giving it a little water spray.

The Bursar took a sliver of wood, shaped like an elongated diamond, and floated it carefully onto the water in the bowl. The pointer aligned itself with the two largest runes on the rim of the cauldron. Satisfied, the Bursar was ready to greet Bol d'Areth as he ambled through the connecting corridor from his office.

Bol d'Areth nodded and harrumphed in a familiar kind of way to Gordon. He took the seat behind the Bursar's desk, beckoning Parry forward. "So, boy, what do you know of your parents – your father, eh?"

Parry shook his head.

"Your mother then. Who was she?" Parry shrugged his shoulders.

"Did they leave you anything?" asked the Bursar. "It's not uncommon for a child to be left with a keepsake, so he may identify his parents later on."

Parry's heart leapt. He had the necklace. He slipped the leather strap over his head and handed it to the Bursar. At last he was to understand its significance. No doubt a token from his mother or father so that they would recognize him one day.

Perhaps the charm had a great power which had kept him safe all these years. Perhaps that was why he had ended up with the world's greatest foster parents. It was the protection his real parents had bestowed upon him.

The Bursar studied the necklace carefully. "It would appear to be one of ours, sir."

The Bol d'Areth raised an eyebrow when he looked at it. The Bursar poured a glass of water and, taking a paperknife from the desk, scraped Parry's amulet of protection. A little powder fell into the glass of water. The glass practically kicked sideways as the water inside it attempted to jump out of the way of whatever the substance was.

"Definitely one of ours," said Gordon.

"You've had this since you were a child?" asked the Bursar.

Parry shrugged. "They gave it back to me when I was fourteen. They said it was with me when I was found."

"Good job they took it away from you. Looks like it was designed to encourage a baby to suck on it. How *lovely*," said Gordon, his voice dripping with irony.

"Curious," said the Bursar. He seemed thoughtful for a moment. "Shall we proceed with the test proper?" It was more of an instruction than a question.

The Headmaster and the Bursar looked to Parry expectantly. After an uncomfortable pause, Gordon leant down to whisper into Parry's ear. "We need a sample of your hair."

Parry barely heard him. His mind was confronting the fact that his mother had clearly wanted to kill him, but clearly didn't believe in doing straightforward things, like throwing him into a river. Hand shaking, Parry plucked a hair from his head and offered it toward the Bursar.

The Bursar rolled his eyes.

Bol d'Areth blew his nose on the sleeve of his robe.

"Not *that* hair," tutted Gordon, donning one of his gardening gloves. "Now hold still." Gordon plunged his hand down the front of Parry's trousers, whipping it back out even faster than it went in.

Parry screamed.

"Oh don't be such a cry-baby," Gordon showed him the pinch of pubic hair he'd retrieved. "It's necessary."

Gordon dropped one or two of the curly hairs into the bowl, and the Bursar added a drop from a phial of thick liquid into the mixture.

The water in the bowl took on a pink hue. The pointer began to revolve slowly on the surface. Everyone looked at it expectantly.

The pointer meandered.

The Bursar blew on it, and it bobbed around a little.

"What's it saying?" Parry couldn't help but ask.

"Not a lot," said Gordon.

The Bursar was looking at the phial, and shaking it. Bol d'Areth snatched it out of his hand, put his little finger in to get a small amount of the liquid and tasted it.

"Aargh!" the Headmaster screwed up his eyes and shook his head about. "No," he said, "that's fine. Well, I'll be damned. Perhaps we should try the other one."

Gordon put the remaining pubic hair in the bowl and the Bursar added a drop from a second phial. This time the pointer suddenly came to rigid attention, centring itself in the bowl, its two ends quivering. Then the leaping and juddering backwards and forwards started.

Even Parry, who no one could claim to be the most perceptive of boys, could read the expression on the wizards' faces.

"It's not supposed to do that, is it?" asked Parry.

Gordon looked at him thoughtfully for a moment. "No. No, it's not supposed to do that."

"How are we doing in the scholarship fund?" Bol d'Areth asked the Bursar without looking at him.

"Very well," said the Bursar. "For the last twenty years annuity rates have been largely favourable, and of course, we haven't actually made an award throughout that period of time."

Bol d'Areth, the master of the harrumph, harrumphed. "Give him a stipend from that then," he said, standing up. "And call together the senior staff. I think they will need to see this." The Headmaster marched off toward his own office.

This left the Bursar and Gordon in the room, together with Parry. The Bursar stared at Parry for a few long moments. Gordon meaningfully cleared his throat.

"Ah yes, of course," said the Bursar. He fished in his pocket for a large brass ring which had a number of keys on it. Moving to one of the cabinets he selected a small key and opened it. He removed a cash chest and placed it on the mantelpiece, and unlocking it he counted out a small number of coins.

He half-closed the lid before Gordon caught his eye. The two of them stared at each other for a few moments, then the Bursar looked back at Parry. He counted out a few more coins, then replaced the chest in its cabinet and locked it, apparently with a completely different key from that which he had used to open it. He whipped a small cloth bag with a drawstring out of an ornamental teapot and dropped the coins into it.

"Twelve and two half-crowns for the semester." The Bursar held the purse in front of him, making Parry walk the few steps to collect it. "That includes your equipment allowance," he said. "You'll find Miss Krasis, the librarian, has an adequate supply of second-hand books and equipment, should you require them."

Parry took the bag.

"Always a pleasure," said Gordon brightly. The Bursar gave him a weak smile, and Gordon led Parry out of the office.

※

Despite being both physically exhausted and emotionally drained, Parry didn't find it easy to get to sleep. This was partly because of the sheer number of narrow scrapes with death he had endured during the day, partly because he had never had so much gold in his possession before, partly because he now knew his real mother had taken a good shake at killing him, but largely it was because he had no idea where his bed was.

and the seamy side of magic

Parry made himself as comfortable as he could in the Sade common room, using two armchairs as a makeshift bed, until by the flickering light of the fire he realized that some of the wall engravings were of rather interesting subjects.

Parry then spent some time studying them, trying to work out a) if the depicted acts were physically possible, and b) whether the acts were still physically possible once he'd worked out the genders of the various participants.

The common room itself was decorated with a wide variety of erotic artworks, bizarre-looking outfits, and what Parry could only guess was torture equipment. There was a rack over in one corner, and chains spaced evenly about the walls. Parry half hoped they were only for decoration, and half hoped they weren't.

It was difficult for Parry to judge the time, his watch being unaccountably missing, but it must have been some hours before the fourth and fifth-formers returned. Most seemed in good spirits, though with some friendly competition in whose welt marks were the most severe.

"Parry!" screamed Hormoany, and then immediately regretted it. He turned to see her putting her hands to her jaw, and wincing.

"You all right, Jude?" asked Parry, calling Hormoany by the nickname she preferred. Parry, at this moment, reckoned he needed a friend.

"Yeah," said Hormoany, clearly distracted by the pain in her face. "Why aren't you dead?"

"Pleased to see you too," replied Parry.

"That didn't come out right," mumbled Hormoany, trying not to move her jaw.

"Well, bugger me with a red-hot poker," greeted Freddie.

"That's not funny," replied Parry.

"I'll say this for you, you certainly know how to beat the odds." An idea had a visibly painful journey across Freddie's face. "Oh rapcus," he swore. "I suppose you'll be wanting to share my room now."

In the darkness the ancient lines flickered, and then glowed in the shape of a pentagram, faintly at first, then slowly growing brighter. The hooded figure chanted: *"Yingtray oti onnectci oury allcim. Easeples ebi atientpai. Yingtray oti onnectci oury allcim. Easeples ebi atientpai."*

A ball of light appeared above the centre of the pentagram, adding its eerie grey glow to that of the lines criss-crossed below. *"Hetum ecipientrum fo oury allcim owsknay ouy rea aitingway. Easeples ebi atientpai. Oury allcim si portantimus oti su. Hetum ecipientrum fo oury allcim owsknay ouy rea aitingway. Easeples ebi atientpai. Oury allcim si portantimus oti su. Easeples oldhus hileway ewi onnectci oury allcim."*

A ghostly face loomed into view in the centre of the foggy ball of light. Distorted, as if viewed inside a goldfish bowl, the face seemed all the more menacing.

"Always," the disembodied voice boomed angrily, "always, when I've just got in the bloody bath. Why is that? Do you wait for me to get in?"

"Forgive me, master," said the cowled figure. "I have news of great import, O master."

The figure in the cloudy globe still seemed to be working some water out of his ear. "You have news of great imports?"

The cowled figure sighed. "Of great *import*, master," he repeated, testily. "The vessel of almighty power has been delivered unto me, that I may deliver it unto thee, that you may overcome your enemies; that with your enemies vanquished and cast down, you might ascend above the leagues of mortals and mages and reign supreme, your will unchallenged for all the ages."

The figure in the shadowy globe finally stopped banging one side of his head whilst waggling a finger in the opposite ear. "There, that's got it," he said. "Now, what are you blathering on about, man?"

The cowled figure sighed. "Your bastard son has arrived. Would you like his blood in liquid form, or would you prefer me to make some sort of black pudding?" he asked dourly.

This got the master's attention. "Really? Who else knows?"

"No other can interpret the signs."

"Good. But we would do well not to underestimate Bol d'Areth or those who serve him. Get me the blood, but try to make it look like an accident, a prank. Distance yourself from the death. Is that clear?"

"I hear and obey, O He-Who-Cannot-Be-Pronounced," declared the cowled figure.

"Yes, yes, yes," said the wizard in the globe. "Just let me know when you've done it. Now, if you don't mind, my bath will be getting cold."

The image of the wizard in the glowing sphere turned and disappeared back into the fog. The sphere itself shrank to a point of light and then disappeared with a loud pop. The servant collected his instruments together. 'Evil masters,' he thought, 'just aren't what they once were.'

CHAPTER 5

It was going to take a while to get the hang of breakfast, but overall it wasn't too bad.

Parry was relieved to see that amongst more dubious dishes there were plenty of breads and cereals, many of which he thought he recognized. But he did have to be careful of the milk-jugs, as they tended to refill themselves as fast as you poured from them, the faulty ones slightly faster. Apparently, someone dropping a juice carafe and forgetting about it had once flooded the Great Hall knee deep.

The first time Parry used a milk-jug, the milk simply spurted out over the table, damping down fried breakfasts of various descriptions. The more particular breakfasters moved away, but Freddie and Hormoany barely seemed to notice.

There was also the distraction of the large drops of water falling from the tarpaulins being arranged high over their heads, to compensate for the missing roof. Floating on broomsticks, school witches and wizards were giving unwanted direction to a number of contractors, themselves mostly using flying carpets as they wove supporting wires across from one side of the roof space to the other and arranged the tarpaulins across them.

It didn't help matters that they tended to do this while sitting on their carpets drinking cups of tea and reading the news. This simply seemed to irritate the school representatives, who buzzed around them, tapping on their newspapers and indicating to the contractors where they might be doing a better job.

"So, what's up with you, faceache?" enquired Freddie Weasel of Hormoany. "Your one kept you talking all night, did she?"

Hormoany didn't seem very amused. She sat with an elbow on the table and her chin in her hand, picking at milk-spattered pancakes.

and the seamy side of magic

"Mine made me scrape the paint off his walls with me teeth, he did," said Freddie, getting to the point of the conversation – himself

"That must have been horrible," said Parry. Something dripped onto his head. Parry glanced up at the postal bats flitting about, and hoped it was only water.

"No, it was all right," Freddie told him. "Got kind of a taste for it after a while. It was real lead paint, none of the namby-pamby fancy modern stuff. And I've got good teeth, me. My granddad was a mountain troll. You need good teeth in the mountain, scraping moss off rocks and armour off travellers."

Parry barely noticed a couple of large drops of water splashing into his bowl.

"So, how did you get on with Vlad?" Freddie asked him. "Did you get the red-hot poker treatment?"

"Oh yeah," replied Parry.

"Hurt, did it?" asked Freddie, fascinated.

"I dunno. Gordon took it off him before he could use it."

"That must have upset him a tad."

"Not half as much as it did when Gordon gave it back to him."

"So why did Gordon come and save you?" Hormoany asked with a minimum of jaw movement. She toyed with her breakfast. "Are you and Gordon...?"

Parry nearly spat his breakfast out. "*No*," he protested through a mouthful of an unidentified cereal. "He just had to take me to see the Headmaster." Parry gave Hormoany a dirty look, and she stared at her pancakes, mentally kicking herself.

"What did old Bol d'Areth want with you, then?" Freddie asked.

"They had this test. It's supposed to let me know who my parents are, for billing reasons, you understand."

"Did they want your blood?" Freddie wanted to know. "It's always blood," he said knowledgeably.

"No, they just ripped some of my hair out," said Parry.

"They tore some hair out of your head?" asked Hormoany.

Parry scratched his head for a moment. "Yes," he said. "That's what they did. They stuck it in this big bowl."

"Cauldron," Hormoany corrected.

"They were testing to see if they could find who my mother was, but this pointer thing on the bowl never did anything."

"Classic!" said Freddie. "A wizard pops into the other world for a bit of how's-your-father with a few tasty mortal types – well, when I say tasty that's frowned upon these days. But hanky-panky – I mean, they're all at it."

"So," said Parry, a little distracted, "so then they tested for my father, and the bloody thing went berserk!"

"You said there was no blood."

"Figure of speech."

"You were getting my hopes up."

"I'm sorry."

"So what did it do, exactly?" asked Hormoany.

"It sort of jumped backwards and forwards, shaking," replied Parry

Hormoany seemed thoughtful. "I've seen something about that. My sister did her dissertation on ancient texts; she was here a couple of years back. I'm sure I could find the book in the library if I tried."

"You enjoy yourself, and while you're doing that, I'll show Parry around the place a bit," suggested Freddie. "You won't want to do a tour of the school with all the first year oiks," he told Parry, nodding towards the group of ten and eleven-year-olds being lined up by a couple of the school prefects. "I'll give you a more personal tour."

"Mm, I could show you round, Parry," offered Hormoany.

"You'll be in the library," interrupted Freddie. Hormoany deflated a little.

"Anyway," continued Freddie, "there's a lot of this school that only I know about, thanks to my brothers." He nodded towards the other side of the hall where the twins were in earnest discussion with a fellow student. Hannibal was suspending the boy by his ankles, and Damian was bending over to have a quiet word in his ear.

"So that's sorted then," said Freddie. "Makes up for the watch."

"Hang on," said Parry.

and the seamy side of magic 97

"Think nothing of it," said Freddie. Then leaning forward looking Parry hard in the eye. "Really. Think nothing of it. I mean it."

Parry glanced at Freddie's brothers and the unfortunate student who was now being used in a game of 'bounce the head off the stone floor'.

"Fair enough," said Parry.

⁂

Warthog School was one of those buildings that had evolved in an ad hoc fashion over a very long period of time – a wing here, an outbuilding there – until it was a sprawling campus of loosely connected buildings. But Freddie, to give him his due, did try to spice up the tour with grisly details about who had died where, when, and in what bizarre fashion. Most of the stories started with how this or that person had upset Freddie's brothers in one way or another…

Bumping into a familiar face on their way round had simply been an unexpected bonus.

Parry held the cupboard doors shut until Freddie returned with the length of chain he'd been looking for. He tied it through the handles, trapping the unfortunate occupant.

"Come on lads," said a voice from the cupboard, "a joke's a joke, okay?"

"So what's all this then?" Parry asked Freddy, ignoring their victim.

"This is the trophy room," said Freddie.

"Let's not talk about the heads," suggested Parry.

Freddie was clearly disappointed. "The heads are the best part. *Heads on sticks*. Not every school's got heads on sticks, you know."

"Still," insisted Parry, "let's not talk about them, eh?"

"Fair enough," said Freddie. "I suppose there'll be time for that when you settle in a bit more."

"What are these?" asked Parry.

"Them there are Kwadwaq brooms."

Parry looked at the brooms in the cases. They looked much like traditional witches' brooms, with bushy twigs at one end, only they tended to have nails or blades or other pieces of metal studded through the handle. Many, if not all of the brooms, were damaged. Some had few twigs left attached, others were split down the middle or snapped in two. All of them looked dented and well used.

"These are some of the finest Kwadwaq players this school has ever had," said Freddie, looking proudly up at a number of portraits on the wall. "That picture there, that was my uncle; this one here, that was my granddad. Not the troll, obviously, the other one."

Parry looked. There was clearly a resemblance. Freddie had the mean look from his granddad's eyes, and his uncle shared the thickset build of Freddie and his two brothers. Parry couldn't help noticing the missing teeth, the lumps and bumps, the field bandages.

"They look like they've been knocked around a bit."

"Well, it's a rough game, is Kwadwaq," agreed Freddie.

"And you fly on these brooms, do you?" asked Parry.

"More like knocked flying," replied Freddie. "Still, you'll have your chance, it's played every week. And in the fifth year you don't have to mess about with those stupid padded brooms, either. It's the real thing. Class. Sheer class.

"Still, we can't hang around here all day," said Freddie, opening the door to the hall. "I've still got to show you the way to the Kwadwaq pitch, the duelling room and, by way of the swimming pool, to the girls' showers."

"We've got a swimming pool here, have we?"

"Well, the pool's dry for the minute. Been dry since Toby Jensen got attacked by sharks."

"You had sharks in the pool?"

"Well, no, not generally," Freddie admitted, "but he hadn't been getting on very well with my brothers..." The door swung shut behind them.

In the cupboard, Goodie Deux-Pantoufles sat wondering what a decent period of time would be before he should start to scream for help.

Freddie's tour finally returned Parry to the relative familiarity of the Sade common room. Parry still didn't have a clear idea of where everything was in the school buildings, but he certainly knew there was a lot of it.

Hormoany was sitting at a table near the rack, her nose in a huge book and her hand in an equally large bag of doughnuts. "Ooh," she said, through half a mouthful of doughnut. "Parry, I think I know what might have been wrong with your test. I think they did it wrong."

Parry was all ears.

"You see, the hair they use…"

Freddie scooped up the doughnut bag, and peered at the contents.

"Well, it shouldn't come from…"

"I don't think that's the problem," interrupted Parry.

"No, you don't understand," said Hormoany. "They should take the hair from…"

"It's all right," Parry cut-in. "They knew what they were doing."

Freddie helped himself to a doughnut, and passed the bag to Parry.

"You see, the hair..." Hormoany continued, oblivious to Parry's darkening expression.

"Look, they knew what they were doing, all right. Just leave it!" Parry took one of the doughnuts.

"No, you see I think they got it wrong. They should have used…"

Parry opted for a blunter course. "Drop it!" he snapped.

"But…"

"Just shut up, okay?"

Parry bit into his doughnut. Clearly it wasn't what he was expecting. He examined the cherry-red filling. "What the hell kind of jam is this?"

"What's jam?" asked Hormoany innocently.

Parry sprayed out his doughnut, as realization and revulsion struck at once.

"Thanks, mate," said Freddie, "but could you try a bit harder? I think there was a guy in the corner you didn't manage to spit on."

Hormoany rescued Parry's once-bitten doughnut from the floor. Dusting it off, she asked, "Does that mean I can have the rest?" She took Parry's frantic tongue-scraping as a 'yes'.

Two familiar figures loomed into view. "All right, Freddie?" greeted Hannibal.

"All right, Jude?" asked Damian, brushing down his sleeve to remove what looked suspiciously like fragments of damp doughnut.

There was a flicker of surprise on the twins' faces when they recognized Parry, who was busy wiping his mouth out with his jacket.

"Parry," said Hannibal, "nice to see you..."

"Alive," finished Damian.

"It's good to see such a select group of our customers," said Hannibal.

"We have some items of quality merchandise which we believe may interest discerning individuals such as yourselves," began Damian, still brushing doughnut fragments and saliva from his sleeve. The twins each took a seat at the table.

"We have here textbooks," said Damian, offering around a number of variously bound tomes. "Always essential for the academic scholar at the start of each new year."

"Hey!" said Parry. "Those are mine!"

Damian's big hand clamped around Parry's outstretched wrist.

"All acquired in good faith, you understand."

Parry hastily agreed while his arm was still in one piece.

"And all available to the previous owner –"

"Or other interested parties," interjected Hannibal.

"– at one bit each."

"Wow!" said Hormoany, delighted with one of the books. "This is really rare, and in such good condition!"

"One bit," said Hannibal, "for these. That one's half-a-crown."

Hormoany bit her tongue.

Parry collected up those books which weren't being jealously guarded by Hormoany.

The Weasel brothers were clearly delighted with off-loading so much stock so quickly.

"We have some other items that our more discriminating clientele might like to acquire." Damian produced a length of rope from his pocket. "Magic rope," he said, "ideal for tying your willing victims…"

"Or unwilling victims," interjected Hannibal.

"…to chairs, beds, or other more specialist pieces of furniture," finished Damian, eyeing the rack in the corner of the common room.

"All at the utterance of the magic word," said Damian.

"What's the magic word?" asked Hormoany, picking up the rope.

"We are prepared to offer a substantial discount on the usual price of these goods," said Damian.

"So what's the magic word?" pressed Hormoany.

"Should you purchase these goods at today's special price…" began Damian.

"…we will make strenuous enquiries of the previous owner on your behalf," continued Hannibal. "Including, but not limited to, séances and Ouija boards."

Hormoany unceremoniously dumped the rope back onto the table.

"We also have an auto-quill," started Hannibal, producing a long, white, battered-looking feather.

"Homework, essays and assignments without the effort," finished Damian.

Parry remembered this item from his first meeting with the twins and immediately reached for it. Hormoany however, still regretting the book incident, snatched it from his hands.

"Well, let's just see, shall we?"

She rummaged in her bag for some ink, then flattened out her empty doughnut bag and requested that the quill write an essay on 'The Theory of Magic'.

The quill hadn't finished the first paragraph when Hormoany humphed and snatched it off the crumpled paper. "Well, that's no good, is it?" she said, handing it back to the Weasels accusingly. "That syllabus hasn't been used since Mr Withershins died."

The brothers looked at one another thoughtfully.

"Wasn't me."

"Me neither."

"I didn't say it was either of you. I just said it's not been used in, what, five or six years? My sister used to do essays like that."

"I can see you have an eye for quality merchandise," said Damian, somewhat disgruntled. He looked at the bag he was carrying, poked around in it for a few moments, and then discarded it. He picked up his brother's, and went through it in the same manner.

"So we have here one or two items which are, without a doubt, of the high quality you so clearly seek. This, for example, is an antique apothecary's set. Said to have once belonged to the wise woman Aneaterm I'Esllay, it contains a coded notebook which may unlock the very secrets of her famed potions d'amour."

"Who would want –" began Parry.

"How much?" snapped Hormoany.

"We couldn't possibly let it go for less than three crowns," said Hannibal.

"I'll give you a crown for it," Hormoany opened the haggling impatiently.

"An item of this value?" Damian shook his head. "Perhaps for the lady we could let it go for two crowns, three half-crowns, two bits and eleven pieces?"

"Very fair," his twin brother commented.

"A crown and a half," snapped Hormoany.

The brothers seemed to consider this. "Make it one crown and three half-crowns," ventured Damian.

"A crown, one half-crown and two bits," responded Hormoany. "Take it or leave it. It's all I've got."

The brothers looked at one another.

"For the lady?"

"If we can trust her discretion. One or two people would be sorely put out if they realized we had offered such an unique piece to Miss Harmonica ahead of them."

"Don't worry, I shan't tell anyone. So, how about it?"

"Done!" The brothers placed the apothecary's set on the table.

"I'm just going to get my money," said Hormoany to Freddie. "Don't let anyone touch these," indicating her books and apothecary's set. She dashed off.

Freddie cast his eye over the apothecary's set. "Some people would be sorely put out, would they?"

"Well, certain people. Like those we flogged the other half-dozen sets to."

Hormoany arrived back, breathless, dipping her hand into a heavy cloth purse and fishing out the required coinage. She counted out the exact money. Anyone who had once dealt with the Weasel brothers tended to do the same.

"I thought you said that was all the money you had," said Damian.

"I distinctly remember hearing that," agreed Hannibal.

Hormoany looked down at the heavy bag, then at the brothers. "I'm on a budget," she said, pulling the drawstrings tight, "and this is spoken for."

"Last but not least," announced Damian, "the choice piece of our collection. The roving eye, complete with crystal ball. Genuine crystal." From impressive-looking velvet bags the glass eye and the crystal ball were produced.

"A demonstration, perhaps?" suggested Damian.

"A demonstration, perhaps," agreed Hannibal.

Damian lifted the roving eye. "*Indfay akednum emalefid leshfos.*" The eyeball levitated from his hand, twisted around, and disappeared through the doorway leading to the girls' dorms.

Hannibal set the crystal ball down in the centre of the table for everyone to view. There was a navel-level image of travel along the corridor, and then the image zoomed in to one keyhole after another. Spotting a young lady in the process of getting changed in one of the rooms, the image reared up, then moved swiftly down and the door swung open.

"Door handles a speciality," commented Damian.

Although the picture was a little distorted by the curvature of the glass, they were clearly watching the back of a half-naked girl as she sorted through her clothes.

She turned and looked past the roving eye to the open door, clutching the dress she was holding to herself. Then she spotted the floating eyeball, and screamed.

"*Eturnra!*" ordered Hannibal.

Immediately the image in the crystal ball blurred as the roving eye rushed back through the corridor to the prospective purchasers.

"And," said Damian, "I think you'll find that as of now we are the sole providers of roving eyes to the Warthogs educational establishment," he said, having checked his wristdial.

"I think you'll find, dear brother, your dial might be a little fast." They compared the wrist-mounted sundials, complete with miniature suns.

"Burstophalies from Midas House," said Freddie, "was knocking them out for one gold crown and two bits, after negotiations."

There was a flash from the window behind the twins. Parry looked out in time to see debris shower from the opposite tower, falling debris – and a falling body.

"I think you're right, brother. A tad fast," said Damian.

"As we were saying," said Hannibal, "as sole providers we're asking a very reasonable four gold crowns."

"Two gold crowns," offered Parry.

"Well, I suppose for an existing customer, we could…"

"Two gold crowns," said Parry. "It's all I've got left."

The twins looked at him. They looked at Hormoany. Then they looked back at him.

"You sure?" asked Hannibal.

"Wouldn't want any mistakes, now would we?" said Damian.

"Straight up," said Parry, offering the two gold coins. "Unless you want me to throw in some of these, of course." He fished a handful of ickstran and ubbishray coins out of his pocket and offered them to the twins.

The brothers looked at the tokens; they looked at the two gold coins; and they looked at each other.

"In the circumstances," said Hannibal, scooping up the gold coins.

"In the exceptional circumstances," agreed Damian.

Parry was presented with the two bags containing the crystal ball and the glass eye.

"Congratulations on your purchase. Complete with user manual," said Damian, handing the document over to Parry. Parry flicked through the hieroglyphs and other unknown languages in which the document was written. "We have a translation available, at a very reasonable cost," said Damian, flourishing a document that was, at least, written in English – largely.

Hormoany had taken the user manual and was inspecting it closely. She was looking at the squiggles which must have been some form of page numbering, and then inspected the inside of the spine closely. "Fourteen pages have been torn out here," she said, after mentally counting.

"And on this occasion we can present it to you free," said Damian, handing Parry the English version of the instructions.

"Just don't tell your friends," said Hannibal.

Damian took Parry by the collar, tightening Parry's jacket painfully around his throat. "Now we do mean that. Don't tell your friends."

"Pleasure doing business with you. We look forward to seeing you again. Hope you have many happy hours' use from your purchases. All transactions final. No refunds," said Damian.

"No recourse," finished Hannibal.

"Will you be attending the soiree this evening?" Hannibal asked Hormoany. Hormoany's defensive posture immediately relaxed.

"Well yes," she said, a smile creeping onto her face.

"Pity," said Damian.

"Still," said Hannibal, "there might be fresh faces."

"Always fresh faces," agreed his brother. Hormoany's face, on the other hand, was looking sour.

ଏଛ

'*Welcome Warthog students old and new,*' read the banner hung above the Great Hall's stage area. An addendum, written on a bed sheet and attached to the main sign, had a long list of students who were specifically unwelcome, and those the Headmaster wished to see. Dead or alive.

By the time Parry, Freddie and Hormoany had arrived at the hall, the evening's welcoming party was well under way. This was partly by design – it never did to turn up early enough to hear the welcoming speeches – and partly by default.

Hormoany had spent an unusual length of time getting herself ready. When asked why it had taken her so long, she said she'd been doing her hair. Freddie suggested she must have been shaving it off and regrowing it from scratch, and received a painful blow to the shin for his trouble.

Despite Parry being unable to see any discernable difference in her hair, there was certainly something different about Hormoany. More attractive, more eye-catching, but it was difficult to put your finger on exactly what.

The hall was already filled with excited first years, who, after listening to the various speeches by their heads of year, had collected timetables and recommended reading book lists. They were now buzzing between the various school club tables, as they sought to invest their excess enthusiasm in organized diversions, where they could make friends and while away the odd evening.

and the seamy side of magic

There were also a fair number of the more predatory older students, largely from Sade and Archer houses, trying to form a few dangerous liaisons with the newbies.

And a fair number who'd only turned up for the grub. Evening meal was cancelled as the Great Hall was in use, so all that was available were sandwiches and the like in the common rooms. Many senior students ventured down here simply to see if the food was any more palatable.

Parry, of course, was wisely suspicious of the finger food, reasoning that on current experience it might actually contain fingers. But he had found some cheese and pineapple on little cocktail sticks, and had loaded-up his plate with those. If he ignored the fact that the cheese had black marbling through it, it tasted good enough.

Gordon, assisted by a couple of sixth-form pupils, was running a surprisingly popular gardening club stall. The popularity was explained by the fact that the first years could entertain themselves by feeding chunks of red meat, and occasionally the tips of their own fingers, to carnivorous plants. The plants snapped hungrily at the morsels on offer, and delighted the children by occasionally burping once well fed.

Freddie was having a heated argument with the people behind the 'Save the Trolls' desk. He wanted to know which trolls, in particular, they would be saving; whether they were relatives of his or not, and whether they would be attempting to save any of the members of several troll clans who, he assured them, were incredibly unpleasant individuals and really did deserve to be broken up with sledge hammers, chisels and pickaxes.

Freddie's brothers were also there, and Parry was surprised to see them behind a desk. The sign above their heads read 'Trading and Commerce Club'.

Damian had quite a respectable list of names of those who had signed up for the club. "So," asked Hormoany, "what exactly is it you do in this club?"

"Well," said Hannibal, "we feel it is our duty..."

"...duty," echoed Damian.

"...our duty to introduce our younger fellows to the ins and outs of the commercial world..."

"Commercial realities," interjected Damian.

"...so as to better provide for their long-term wealth and welfare," finished Hannibal.

"Which day do you meet?" asked Hormoany suspiciously.

The twins glanced at one another, and then back at Hormoany.

"That has yet to be decided," replied Damian.

"And this commercial acumen you bestow on your club members," continued Hormoany, "this comes at a price, does it?"

The twins exchanged an irritated look.

"One half-crown is hardly excessive for the lessons we can teach the new students. It doesn't do, you know, for them to remain financially naïve throughout their schooling, now does it?"

"So," said Hormoany, thinking it through, "you take half-a-crown from each of your applicants" – Hannibal nodded – "and then you never hold a meeting of any sort."

Damian leant forward. "A small price for such a valuable lesson, I think we can all agree," he hissed. "Now, unless you'd like to join…"

Hormoany huffed.

"Is there something different about you tonight, Jude?" asked Hannibal, changing the conversational tack.

Hormoany was momentarily disarmed.

"Oh, it's that new conditioner you know. How nice of you to notice," she preened.

"It's good, that, whatever it is she's using," said Damian.

"Tell me," asked Hannibal, "are you rubbing it on your hair, or pouring it into your bra?"

Hormoany chose to leave the twins table, turning on her heels and striding away in a strop. She led the amused Parry and Freddie over to the 'Amateur Dramatics' club. It seems she'd been very active in the costume making, and she mentioned proudly how she had dressed many of the leading actors and actresses, not to mention the stage.

Hormoany explained that, much as she would like to act, there were so few people who could make new costumes, and so many who thought they were great actors and actresses.

"Not good enough," mouthed Freddie, pointing at Hormoany, and got an elbow in the ribs for his troubles.

The school apparently boasted two newspapers, which had chosen to set up at opposite ends of the hall. The staff of '*The Sol*' were boasting of their daring lithographs, their 'man of the people' standards, and their investigative journalism which had recently seen the smashing of an illegal potions smuggling ring.

'*The Epoch*', on the other hand, prided itself on its high ethical standards and unbiased commentary, and was leading with an article about how its former editor had been framed by '*The Sol*'; how the two prosecution witnesses just happened to own large stakes in the rival newspaper, and how they enjoyed quite a high turnover in illicit magical articles themselves.

Possibly the most eye-catching display was that of the 'Crystal Healing Club'. Hormoany listened intently as the various stones, energy lines and healing properties were explained. Freddie, on the other hand, seemed less impressed.

In a magical world Parry would have been willing to give the crystals the benefit of the doubt. Sure, in his own world, they were an invented cure for invented maladies which seemed to strike down people who had too much time on their hands, but surely in this magical world...

Freddie leaned forward and said – in a whisper that could quite easily carry from one side of the hall to the other – "Barking! Absolutely barking! Still, it keeps them off the streets."

Freddie's opinion of the 'Battlefields and Tanks Club' was hardly any higher. Apparently they enthusiastically donned camouflage outfits and pushed large wooden tanks around sports fields, pretending to shoot at one another.

Freddie could have understood it if at least they'd been in caves, but throwing over-sized dice with apparently random numbers of sides on the sports field didn't seem to him to be something that sane people did.

The 'Toad and Newt Keeping Club' and the 'Cookery Club' appeared to have a symbiotic relationship. One seemed to raise toads and newts largely as a raw ingredient for the other. However, the large cookbook with the title 'A Thousand and One Ways with Rats' would have been more than enough in itself for Parry to have given both the stalls a wide berth.

The tapping of a spoon on a crystal wineglass called the hall to attention.

A senior wizard, Artorius Smudge, stood upon the stage. "Now the moment you've all been waiting for. One of those occasions, one of those moments that you'll remember for the rest of your life," he declared pleasantly, smiling benignly at the first years.

"Behold!" he said, "the house ghouls!" The curtains drew themselves back, revealing the other three housemasters and four glowing pentagrams. Within each pentagram the amorphous figure of a ghoul could be seen.

Various shades of grey and green, the ghouls hovered like small malevolent clouds, their eyes jumping between the people in the hall, trying to select a victim. Short, clawed arms and their sharp teeth somehow seemed more real than the rest of their bodies. They hissed and crackled as they strained the bounds of their magical enclosures.

"Each year, as you know," announced Artorius in a theatrically grave voice, "the ghouls are permitted to take the life of one new and unwary pupil from their own house, as a lesson to those who would face danger unprepared."

The first years oohed and aahed at the right points during the speech. "Will it be you?" asked Artorius, pointing at a child who cringed as his fellows laughed; "Or you?" pointing at a girl who squealed as her friends giggled. "Flee while you can, or let your magic face its first deadly test!"

Artorius began the count which was taken up by the senior pupils. "Ten, nine, eight…" The first years fled, "seven, six, five…" Parry watched as they pushed their way out of the hall, giggling and shouting and screaming. "Four, three, …"

"They're not actually dangerous, are they?" asked Parry, reassured by the fact that Freddie had resumed his argument

and the seamy side of magic 111

with both the Crystal Healers and the Save the Troll delegations, who had now abandoned their stalls and were collecting as many sandwiches as they could find.

Hormoany was attempting a world record, both in the number of goodies she could pile onto her plate and into her mouth at the same time.

"No, not really dangerous," Hormoany assured Parry as she popped a couple more sandwiches into her mouth. "Humph, humph, humph hrrr!"

"Two, one, one half! Gentlemen, release the ghouls!" cried Artorius.

Each of the housemasters stretched a tentative foot forward, and shuffled a little of the chalk markings away. The instant the pentagram was broken the ghouls were released. They sprang like greyhounds from the traps, a couple shooting directly for the fleeing first years as the last of them escaped through the door. The two others, zigzagging high around the hall, were making in the same general direction.

At the door, one of the ghouls paused, and cast an eye back over what ought to have been its shoulder.

One of the boys from the 'Save the Troll Society' had suggested that the trolls from Ragmount Ridge might not be worth saving and, rather than this being the peace offering towards Freddie he had intended, the boy found himself pushed up against a wall with Freddie demanding to know what he was implying about his grand-ma.

Parry directed his question towards the back of Hormoany's head. "So, they wouldn't actually hurt anybody?"

"They used to get one or two every year," she began. "Ooh, are those Eve's apples? Mmm. Humph, humph hrrr!"

"Do what?" asked Parry.

"Humph herrumph-humph, humfefhumph!" said Hormoany.

"Sorry, I don't speak 'piglet' – er, what's everybody looking at?" Parry interrupted himself.

It had seemed to go very quiet. Freddie was still holding the 'Save the Trolls' activist clear off the ground – his fist poised to strike again – but he was looking back towards Parry, as was his captive who was making no attempt to struggle.

Parry got that sense that he was being watched, eyes burrowing into the back of his head. Possibly the hot snorting breath on the back of his neck was giving it away. He turned, slowly. Hovering malevolently behind him was a large greenish-grey ghoul.

They were mostly harmless, Parry reminded himself. "There's a good ghoul," he said, uncertainly.

The ghoul, as much as an amorphous cloud with teeth and arms can, seemed quite pleased with itself. A very solid, slimy tongue snaked out and slapped into Parry's face. He raised his hands to protect himself, the slime splattering his neck and one cheek, and worse still, a little got into his mouth. "Ugh, that's disgusting!" he spat. "Shoo, shoo, go on. Clear off!"

But the ghoul seemed not to want to shoo, and drew back its cloudy lips, its sharp yellowy teeth snapping at Parry's arm.

It was reflex alone that saved Parry from losing his hand. The ghoul's sharp teeth still caught his jacket, shredding the sleeve. It seemed to find the material as distasteful as Parry had found the slime, spitting out the cloth and picking fibres from its tongue and teeth.

Its eyes then turned back to its intended victim. It smiled in the way a shark might smile at a hapless bather and – in a moment of pure understanding between hunter and prey – Parry screamed an obscenity and leapt up onto the table which afforded him his only escape route clear of other people.

Hormoany was traumatised. "Not the food!" she screamed as Parry tore through a selection of appetisers and desserts.

The ghoul appeared to chuckle. It rose above the heads of the startled assembly in the hall, until it saw Parry reach the door. As Parry reached the doorway, the ghoul swooped down.

The chase was on.

The ghoul had a few distinct advantages over Parry. For one, it could fly; for two, it could pass through solid objects when it chose; and for three, it knew its way around the school.

Parry was the new boy, and it was his first attempt at running across the magical junctions in the school.

Freddie had demonstrated that the speed you crossed these thresholds tended to dictate where in the school you reappeared.

and the seamy side of magic

If you strolled, you just got where you were going. If you went a bit faster, you might find yourself at other end of a corridor. At the headlong dash Parry was making – well, it was anybody's guess where he would turn up.

One instant he was pelting down a wide, main, well-lit corridor. The next second he was at another end of the building, on the first floor, in a dark, narrow corridor.

And although the ghoul couldn't take advantage of the shortcuts, it did seem to know exactly where Parry would reappear – sometimes floating up behind him to say 'Boo!' – sometimes waiting for him around a corner with a little 'cooey' wave.

Parry crept down the darkened corridor, his eyes scanning this way and that for a door. Walking into a suit of armour he nearly scared himself to death.

Lights filled the corridor as an office door was opened, and a wizard came rushing out. "What the hell do you think you're doing, boy?"

It was Jape, the wizard Parry had bumped into with Freddie and Hormoany at the coffee house in Xfordo Reetsti.

Parry saw the greenish glow as the ghoul rose up the stairwell and emerged into view. "There it is, there it is!" screamed Parry. "Help me! He's after me!"

Jape had one hand on his stomach, with the other he was supporting himself against a pillar. "Why," he asked through gritted teeth, "should I care?"

Jape tipped forward, half striding and half falling back into his office, slamming the door behind him.

Parry beat uselessly on the door. "Please, he's coming! For pity's sake!"

The ghoul advanced down the darkened corridor, enjoying the scene, savouring it, running a slimy tongue across its amorphous lips and very morphous teeth.

Parry pointed his wand at the apparition: "No, no!" he cried, channelling his fear through the wand. This had an immediate affect upon the ghoul.

Apparently, it tickled.

Parry backed away. Suddenly his foot caught on something, sending him tripping backwards. He hit the ground heavily, but not so heavily that he didn't recognize what he had fallen over.

Parry made a grab for the sword posed with the suit of armour. He tugged at it and tugged at it. The empty metal gauntlet seemed unwilling to give up the blade. In desperation Parry kicked at the suit of armour. The armour fell one way, and the sword and Parry fell the other.

Parry picked himself up. At least now he had a solid weapon. The ghoul kept advancing.

"Stay away from me," cried Parry, brandishing the sword. "I'm warning you!"

Parry tried a few practice swings with the sword, knocking sparks off the stone wall on one side of the passage, and smashing jars and windowpanes on the other. The ghoul shot forward and stopped in the air just a few feet in front of Parry. It appeared to be presenting itself to him.

"Right," said Parry, "I warned you!" And he swung the sword.

It cut through the ghoul from its top left side to its bottom right. Parry swung the sword again, this time bringing it down through the middle of the ghoul's head, between its eyes, through its mouth, until the blade struck ground.

Parry might just as well have tried to hack apart the mist.

The ghoul smiled.

Parry ran.

There was a door at the end of the corridor. He snatched it open, ran through, and slammed it shut, still dragging the sword behind him. The French windows across the room were locked. He threw himself hard against them, once, twice, three times.

The face of the ghoul started pushing itself through the door Parry had just slammed shut. Parry threw himself one more time at the windows. They gave way, bursting open. Parry and sword fell through – and kept falling.

Parry's momentum had taken him straight over a low balcony rail, and out into freefall. He crashed hard into the undergrowth, but the bushes at least saved his life. Or possibly more accurately, extended it for a couple more minutes.

and the seamy side of magic 115

The wind knocked out of him, Parry couldn't reply to whoever it was complaining: "Ow! That bloody hurt! Where the hell did you come from? What little idiot goes throwing himself off balconies at this time of night? I'm sure you've broken something, maybe several somethings. Now what am I going to do? Your spectacles are by your elbow, by the way."

Parry couldn't answer. He had rolled himself over onto all fours and, having retrieved his glasses, was crawling away as best he could.

Using the sword to lean on, he dragged himself back to his feet and pushed his way through the plants and bushes. At least if he stayed close to the building, and within the cover of the foliage, he might be hidden from the ghoul for a few moments.

The bushes soon thinned out. Now he recognized where he was.

He was towards the back of the building where the sports changing rooms, pavilion, workshops and magical testing areas were. Maybe he could hide out here somewhere.

He looked, but couldn't see the ghoul's glow. He started running along, following the wall, looking for a way back in.

There was a door. He tugged at the handle. He turned it. He pushed. He pulled. He banged on it, but it was hopeless. The door was a solid external door, and it was bolted shut. And then, not more than a hundred paces from him, was the ghoul, glowing, enjoying the sight of a meal tenderised by a fall.

The ghoul was advancing, picking up speed. Parry was backing off. There was nowhere to hide, nowhere to run.

The ghoul accelerated.

Crack! Crack! The bolts inside the door were thrown back and the heavy metal door swung open, into the path of the ghoul. The Bursar stepped out, and caught sight of Parry.

The ghoul burst straight through the metal door as if it wasn't there, but struck the Bursar as you might expect one solid object to strike another. The ghoul recoiled. It sounded as though it caught its breath with fear.

The Bursar, knocked to the ground, rolled, and with cat-like agility regained his feet, his wand at the ready. "*Egonebium iciousvay engreous oudclay!*"

Sparks flew from the Bursars wand. Scalded by the spell the ghoul cried out in a terrible inhuman pain, and fled skyward, disappearing over the chimneystacks.

The Bursar turned to Parry. "What's wrong with you, child? Don't you even know the simplest protection spell?" The wizard raised his wand. *"No orfum oulghae onsumptioncus."*

Parry jolted as the spell hit him, but felt no pain.

"Oh, it's you, Hotter. I would have expected Gordon to be more careful with those he goes to all the effort to trawl in." The Bursar looked back toward the school building and shook his head at the disappointed faces pressed against the windows. "I fear I have spoilt the show."

The Bursar slammed the heavy metal door, and tapping it with his wand, heard the bolts slide back into place. He looked back at Parry, sitting stunned on the grass. He tutted, turned on his heel and marched towards the main building.

Parry slumped backward, feeling unable to move, the heavy fall catching up with him.

But then there was another noise. The Bursar's footsteps had disappeared, but there came the clunk! clank! clunk! clank! of heavy metallic footsteps echoing towards him. Clunk! Clank! Clunk! Clank!

'This is it,' thought Parry, 'whatever it is. I'll just give up now. I'll just lie here, and hope it's all over soon.'

Clunk! Clank! Clunk! Clank! A silhouetted figure loomed into view, and bent over him. A hollow voice boomed, "Mine, I think." It reached down.

Parry watched a metal gauntlet as it snatched up the sword from the grass. "And they're going to expect *me* to hammer the kinks out, I'll wager," complained the suit of armour as it trudged back toward the building.

Parry thought that a very good moment to lose consciousness.

CHAPTER 6

The crystal ball misted as it was breathed on, then jiggled about as a jacket sleeve roughly polished it. The images in the ball remained dim and indistinct.

"Are you sure it's working?" Parry asked.

"Yeah, yeah," said Freddie. "It's probably just moving too fast. Hang on, I think it's slowing down."

Sure enough, the images in the crystal ball became less blurred, a little more focused; they were looking down on treetops from maybe twice the height of the trees themselves.

"Are you sure about all this ritual dancing?" Freddie asked Hormoany.

"Of course I'm sure," answered Hormoany. "I sat next to Alicia in astrology last year, and her friend Diana's sister is a witch. She said the sixth-form witches do it every year on the first day of term, sort of bless the school to bring good fortune."

"And they dance naked?" queried Freddie. "Are you sure?"

"Of course I'm sure!" Hormoany snapped. She did not like to have her wisdom questioned. "It's so they can be as one with the skies and the earth."

"Dirty perverts," said Parry, with relish.

"If they're so dirty, why did you want to watch it then?"

There was an uncomfortable pause.

"Purely educational," suggested Freddie.

"Yeah, educational," agreed Parry. "Anyway, you wanted to watch it too."

"I have a genuine interest in ritual and sympathetic magic," said Hormoany, avoiding the boys' gaze by staring hard at the crystal ball.

"Look, I think it's found them!"

The image in the crystal ball zoomed in over the trees towards some wispy white smoke. Hovering above a clearing, it rotated down to reveal a small wood fire and the loosely grouped figures below.

"What are they doing?" hissed Parry, as if afraid he'd be overheard by the coven they were spying on.

"Not a lot," replied Freddie, staring into the ball.

"They're probably waiting for the right moment," suggested Hormoany.

"And when *is* the right moment to get your kit off?" wondered Freddie aloud.

"Shhh! Look!" said Hormoany. "Something's happening!"

Indeed, one figure had donned antlers and had raised his arms into the air. Casting off their robes, the coven linked hands around the fire, which suddenly blazed brightly.

"Wheyhey!" enthused Parry.

They watched the figures silently cavort, until the smoke began to interfere with their view.

"Back it off a little," said Hormoany.

"Just trying to find the right words," said Freddie. He practised a few magical phrases until he managed to find the right one. The image in the crystal ball became clear again, as the roving eye backed out of the way of the smoke.

"They're even further away now," complained Parry.

"Mm," agreed Hormoany. "Can we zoom in?"

"I'll try, said Freddie, checking his notes, "*Indfay akednum emalefid leshfos.*"

Suddenly the roving eye stopped moving backwards and zoomed in onto the crowd. "Oh, no!" exclaimed Parry. "It would have to be *her*, wouldn't it?"

"Well, the eye can't help it," said Freddie. "After all, I told it to find naked flesh. It's simply gone to the person with the largest surface area."

"Lock it onto the next person," said Parry.

Freddie issued the command, "*Extnay easeples,*" and the eye refocused.

"Oh, that's much better!" enthused Hormoany.

"That really *has* put me off my breakfast," complained Parry.

"I think it's rather nice," said Hormoany.

Parry looked at Freddie. "Can't you move it on to a female?" he pleaded.

"I'm trying, I'm trying," said Freddie, experimenting with a few more commands.

The image leapt to the next in the circle. "Ooh, that's Miss Mandrake," recognised Hormoany. "She lectures in medicinal herbs, and midwifery. She's quite sprightly, you've got to admit, for ninety-odd."

"I may not be able to eat for the rest of the day," complained Parry.

"Hold on! What's happening?" asked Freddie.

"Quick, they've spotted the eye!" cried Hormoany. "Call it back!"

"*Eturnra!*" shouted Freddie. The roving eye narrowly escaped the palm of a hand that was coming straight towards it.

"That was a close one," said Parry.

"If they'd grabbed the eye," said a relieved Freddie, "they might have been able to spot us, if they know how to reverse the sight."

"Well, I thought that was a really useful exercise," said Hormoany.

"Only because you got to ogle that sixth-form boy," commented Freddie.

"And what did *we* get?" complained Parry. "The Goodyear blimp, and the prune that the grave forgot."

"Still, not a bad first attempt," said Freddie.

The sharp crack of breaking glass announced the return of the roving eye.

"Okay," demanded Freddie, "what berk shut the window?"

༺༻

"I still reckon," said Parry, giving up on the remains of his breakfast, "that we should send it to the girls' showers next time."

Freddie considered this. "There's always the fogging-up problem. Perhaps if we warmed the roving eye first, and then maybe some rubbing alcohol…"

"You're not sending it over there while *I'm* in the showers," said Hormoany sternly.

"Course not," agreed Freddie. "We've had enough of a fright as it is."

Anticipating the reaction, Freddie was just fast enough to dodge Hormoany's spoon.

Hormoany decided she'd talk to Parry instead.

Parry was busy reading the letter from his foster parents they had found outside his bedroom door. It had been attached to the suitcases Hormoany had fallen over as she'd led the dash down to breakfast. Although Parry had only waded through the first three of the twelve pages, it seemed they were surprised at his decision to join the *French Foreign Legion*, and were taking this opportunity to apprise him on their views of the morality of war.

"I think I've turned up some really interesting information about your parental test," Hormoany announced to Parry, breaking his concentration.

"Yeah," Parry said, "what, then?"

"I think," said Hormoany in hushed tones, "that you have two wizard fathers."

"Do what?" said Parry, surprised. With the others, he stood up and started wandering to the Great Hall's door.

"Two fathers," repeated Hormoany. "I found some references in a handful of texts. My sister did her dissertation on Ancient Prophecy, and I knew that I'd seen something in there about this, so I looked it up, and there it was in a footnote. So I followed the reference, and look, I've got this prophecy."

"It's in gibberish," said Parry, looking at the scrap of paper Hormoany offered.

"It's the ancient tongue," she explained. "I haven't been able to translate all of it yet, but I think it refers to another prophecy. I won't know until I've finished the translation and found any references. A lot of the prophecies are like that, referring back one to the other."

"That's not possible, is it?" wondered Freddie, lagging behind the conversation somewhat.

"What's not possible?" asked Parry.

and the seamy side of magic

"Two dads? I mean how would you...? Where would you...?"

"Don't even think about it," said Parry. "Does it say anything about my mother?" he asked Hormoany

"No, that's just the thing. I don't think you had a mother, as such."

"You've got to be kidding me. This is a wind-up, isn't it?"

"No," said Hormoany. "Honestly, it's all in the texts."

"Yeah, right," said Parry, pushing back to Hormoany the note with gibberish on it. "I don't think you can be looking in the right places, thank you very much."

ೞ

Parry, Freddie and Hormoany waited with the rest of the class in the hall outside Artorius Smudge's lecture room. A couple of sixth-formers obligingly decided to air their dirty laundry a little further down the corridor, providing everyone with a little entertainment while they were waiting.

"And I suppose you don't remember giving me this, either?" the girl accused, pulling down the neck of her dress in order to show the bright red bite mark.

"I don't know what the hell potions you were on," replied the boyfriend, "but I was at Kwadwaq practice all night and then out with the lads. What sort of girl picks up a complete stranger and then boasts about it to her boyfriend in the morning? Oh yes, I'm sorry, I forgot. You *are* in Sade House, aren't you?"

"You slimy toe-rag!" snapped the girl. "That's the last time..."

"Thank you," said Artorius Smudge, silencing the arguing couple. Embarrassed, they slipped away. Smudge watched them go before opening up the classroom.

Artorius smiled and nodded benevolently as his students filed past. "Pleased to see you, pleased to see you. Do sit down, do sit down. Yes."

The chairs in the room were clearly enchanted. As an apprentice approached a desk, the chair would pull itself out and then tuck itself back in as they went to sit down.

"Hurry up! Come along!" said Artorius. "Everybody here?"

He looked down at the register, which ticked itself off. "Excellent," he said. "Today is your first lesson in the contemporary history of magic." As if in a conventional if old-fashioned schoolroom, Artorius chalked up the main points as he spoke. A little unconventionally, he wasn't actually holding the chalk as he did so.

"Those of you who attended my lessons last year," continued Artorius, and Parry was sure he glanced at him, "will remember the near stalemate that was reached in the Mage Wars, largely as the main protagonists – Eplerk, Eynmanfus, Instiene, Raussk, Rodingersch, Ubbleh to name but a few – did not enjoy risking themselves in outright combat, and so fought largely by proxy. Eplerk, Instiene and Ubbleh held the highlands and eastern lowlands, Raussk held the mountains and valleys to the south and so forth.

"The midland region was largely stabilized by the unconventional alliance of Archer, Sade, Midas and Canute, and their establishment of their Warthog base training camp – designed to raise an army with which to do battle against the other mages – the original establishment upon which, of course, this school was founded.

"Now, who can give me a precedent for such an alliance between sorcerers, hmm?"

A handful of arms went up. Artorius consulted his attendance register. "Hotter."

Parry sat very still for a few moments, then shook his head.

"Ah, I see," Artorius said, pleasantly enough. "Mm." He made a mark in the register, then asked another student.

"Oh, when Ildew and Arlowem got together to raise a magical army."

"That's right," agreed Artorius. "In which year?"

"31,281," offered another student.

"Very close," said Artorius in a kindly fashion. "31,281 was when their alliance dissolved."

"Who remembers when they got together? Yes, 31,229, when the forces of Ildew and Arlowem were separately defeated in battle with an unknown foe who decimated the apprentice forces each had managed to raise.

"So, despite there not being any successful precedent for this alliance, the training camp was indeed formed and held together for three years – until what happened? Hotter?"

Parry was again on the spot, and it occurred to him that if he had actually read any of the books salvaged from the collection that Gordon had given him, he might now be in a better position. He shook his head.

Artorius marked the register again. "Harmonica?"

Hormoany was only too pleased to answer the question. "That was the arrival of Bol d'Areth, sir."

"Quite right, quite right," concurred Artorius, "the great vanquisher himself."

"What do we know of Bol d'Areth up to this point, Hotter?" asked Artorius.

Parry had to shrug.

Artorius marked the register. "I see, well never mind. You'll soon catch up, eh? Weasel?"

Freddie woke up. "Well, he'd done in every bugger he'd laid his hands on."

"I prefer to say," corrected Artorius, "that Bol d'Areth was undefeated in what we now know to be at least twenty-five magical contests, with some scholars putting the possible number as high as sixty, including witches and warlocks, lesser mages and sages.

"Does anyone recall the original reason for his rampage? Yes, Smith?"

"The sorcerer Zeladin had demanded tithes from his land."

"Yes," said Smudge. "And what about this particularly annoyed Bol d'Areth?"

Another student volunteered: "That the tithe collector arrived on a Sunday, when Bol d'Areth liked a lie-in?"

"Yes, quite right. One of our more strictly observed school rules is never to bother the Headmaster on a Sunday morning. Now," said Artorius, warming to his topic, "who remembers when we first met Bol d'Areth's apprentice..."

The second lesson was, if possible, even worse.

Parry did his best to ignore the sniggering that was going on amongst some of the other pupils. Surely, he thought, the fact he hadn't got such a wide grasp of magical history wasn't that funny. And it would have been something of a relief to see the master arrive, were it not Jape.

Parry wondered if his continual sour mood were influenced by the fact that he seemed forever to have some sort of stomach ache. Parry couldn't help but hope that it was an inflamed appendix, and that it would burst soon.

The most notable feature, as the pupils filed into Jape's dungeon-like classroom, was the statue of a student in the back row.

"Strewth," whispered Freddie, "I thought that was just a rumour. They said he'd changed one of his pupils to stone for playing up in the lesson, but I didn't think he'd still be here."

"What," said Parry, "he's been here all summer?"

"Yeah," said Freddie, "boy, that man holds a grudge."

"This lesson," announced Jape, "is in the art of transfiguration. Transfiguration is *real* magic. It's not the namby-pamby stuff you might play with in other lessons. It is powerful, and it is dangerous.

"Therefore, there will be no talking in my lesson, there'll be no coughing, sneezing or fidgeting. No one will touch a wand unless I say so, and no magic words are to be uttered – other than those I have expressly identified – and then only upon the targets I have specified. Anyone breaking the least of my rules will spend the rest of the day as a toad. Is that clear?

"You will note you each have some sand in front of you. Today's first lesson – an easy one – will be to transform sand into stone."

Freddie leant over toward Parry. "At least he's in a good mood."

Lunchtime of his first academic day at Warthogs was something of a quiet affair for Parry. Freddie had disappeared, presumably off to the lake or the moat. Hormoany had insisted she go back to the library to continue her research regarding Parry's parentage.

That left Parry to mooch about, out of the way as much as possible of other students who, he would swear, were talking about him behind his back. It was the way they would giggle and laugh, and when he looked around they would immediately look away.

So half the long lunchtime – wizards it seemed, preferred at least a couple of hours to enjoy their food – Parry spent sunbathing near the sports pavilion, waiting to see students he recognized roll up for the afternoon's sports lesson, Kwadwaq.

Parry had to admit he was hoping he'd be able to make his mark in this sport. He was a pretty mean football player – mean in the sense that if you didn't surrender the ball to him, he would put you out of the game with tackles rarely seen outside of a streetfighter movie – so he had to hope the skills were transferable.

And, hey, despite the fact that Jape appeared to hate everyone, and him in particular, and that he'd had to work on his own during the lesson, Parry had at least been able to make his sand clump together.

Obviously, there were the Judicita Harmonicas of this world, who had turned their sand into a smooth stone tablet, and had got as far as engraving their initials on it, but Parry was content to have achieved anything on his first try.

Sure enough, once he'd waited for a while, he recognized a number of the people from his previous two classes as they entered the pavilion, and he followed them in.

Grenadier Gardner, the sports master, had a voice like a sergeant major, and believed if he wasn't shouting at his pupils they weren't benefiting from his experience. Therefore, he shouted a lot.

This even hastened Parry's wary climb into his Kwadwaq outfit, basically a lightweight version of wizarding robes, stopping just below the knee and halfway between his elbow and wrist. And Parry's general feeling of paranoia wasn't helped much when one of the students wandered up and asked, "Are you Hotter – Parry Hotter?"

"Yeah," said Parry. "I'm new here. What's *your* name?"

But the apprentice simply turned to his friend and said "Told yer!" And they both laughed and left.

"Come on! Come on!" Grenadier Gardner was yelling. "On to the pitch! Hup, hup, hup!"

"Gribbin and Foster, broom duty!" he snapped, opening a cupboard and handing one boy a rolled-up piece of carpet and the other an armful of brooms.

Parry trudged out to the Kwadwaq field, along with the others. The carpet, hovering a little off the ground, was carrying the brooms. Gribbin and Foster were ensuring that any which rolled off were put back on, promptly.

When Parry reached it, he saw that the pitch itself was an elongated oval with what looked like a small goal at either end, roughly the size you might see in hockey. There was a halfway line marked and a centre circle, with two additional lines either side of the circle's halfway point.

It was on these lines, roughly two paces apart, that Grenadier Gardner lined up the two arbitrary teams. It was around now that Parry realized that nobody might actually be about to tell him how Kwadwaq was played.

Gribbin and Foster had gone down the line handing out the battered school broomsticks. At least these had no nails or blades in them. But what exactly were you supposed to do? How were you supposed to play?

"Okay people," shouted Grenadier Gardner. "Listen up. We're going to play four ten-minute halves, get the old hand-eye co-ordination working again after the break. This is just a friendly game so we can see where the talent is, and where the skills may unfortunately be lacking.

"On three," he said, holding above his head what looked like a large ball bearing. "One, two," there was a short, sharp blast on the whistle –

'Hey, but I don't' – Parry's thought process was interrupted by his brain bouncing off the inside of his skull. He was

and the seamy side of magic 127

vaguely aware of what must have been a painful impact across the side of his face and his head, were he not blissfully anaesthetized by the sudden disconnection from four of his five senses. He saw the ground disappear, and the sky rush past, before he hit the turf and lost the last of those senses.

§

Parry slowly regained consciousness.

He became aware that he was in a bed, and that his head hurt, especially the left-hand side.

Experimentally he opened the one eye which was not swollen shut. The light above his head swung round violently, so Parry chose to think the experiment was unsuccessful and shut it again.

"Urrghh!" he groaned.

He heard a concerned voice. The voice was familiar, but Parry couldn't quite place it. "Are you awake?" it asked.

"Does it hurt when you're awake?" asked Parry.

"Generally," said his companion.

"Then I must be awake." Parry opened his eye again. The light swung at a more leisurely pace.

"Everyone's been quite worried about you, you know. You've been out cold for about three hours. That Grenadier Gardner brought you in himself. Said you didn't take guard on the pike-line. Rookie mistake in Kwadwaq, so I'm told.

"I'm in here because of a fall. Some berk fell on me. Damn near turned me into matchwood." Parry was now certain the voice was familiar.

"Gordon's been in, even the Bursar looked in to see how you were. Wanted to be informed the minute you stopped breathing, something about collecting residual sums. But don't worry, Mr Tollopoff is looking after you. He's the best in the business."

Hormoany stuck her head round the curtain.

"Hiya, Jude!" said Parry. "Oh great, you've brought food."

Hormoany looked puzzled for a moment, and then realized. She looked down at the wicker box she was carrying under a book of material samples. "Oh, no, Parry. You really did get hit very hard, didn't you?"

She put the box on a spare chair and sat down, opening the lid and tipping the box towards Parry for him to look in. Inside the box sat the biggest toad he had ever seen. It had a stony hide, and a somehow familiar face.

"Oh," said Parry, "all right, Freddie?"

The toad gave no indication that it had understood.

"He might be better by teatime," said Hormoany. "Or possibly midnight." She put the basket lid back down. "It seems to calm him," she said.

The curtain around Parry's bed was pulled back by a man wearing what could only be described as a carpenter's apron, complete with sawdust and tools, and a stethoscope around his neck.

"Oh, we're awake, are we? My name's Tollopoff, and I understand you're Parry Hotter. Good to see you back with us."

Tollopoff sat next to Parry.

"Now," he said, "just follow the light." He took out a little pen-like instrument and pointed it at Parry.

"Aarrgh!" screamed Parry. "My eye! My eye! I can't see!"

Tollopoff looked at the pen he was using. "I do beg your pardon. That's not my torch at all, it's my laser pointer. Still, that's exactly the right reaction, to a laser. I think you'll be fine."

"What the hell kind of doctor are you?" demanded Parry.

"Well, I'm not a doctor as such," admitted Tollopoff. "It's terribly complicated, but I think it revolves around the difficulty of getting qualified staff who will work here. I'm a tree surgeon, by trade. Simply got roped into it, really, and it's quite a fun job. Obviously, the plants keep me busy most of the time, but I don't mind helping out where I can, especially as Gordon seems to have most things in order. How's your vision?"

"I've got these great big dark grey blobs wherever I look with this eye. The one I can open."

"Oh, exactly what we'd expect, when someone's had a laser shining in their eye from such a short range. Quite normal. If full vision hasn't return in a day or two pop back. I'll see what I can do."

Hormoany helped Parry get out of the bed and find his glasses. He was blinking heavily. "I think I'll be a lot safer anywhere but here," he told Hormoany.

"Are you off then?" asked the voice from the next bed.

"Yeah," replied Parry. "I know you think he's something, but it seems a bit dangerous to me."

"Oh, don't worry about it – he's brilliant. Fix you up in no time. I'd give that man any limb he wanted."

"Really," said Parry, doubtfully.

Tollopoff came back with a small hacksaw and a pot of resin. "No rest for the wicked, eh?" He pulled back the curtain on the other bed.

Behind the curtain, sitting in a large wooden wheelbarrow was – well – a bush.

"Nice chatting with you then, Parry," called the bush. "See you around, maybe."

It was fortunate for Parry's mental health that, as he squinted around to say goodbye, he put the fact that he didn't see who was speaking down to his near blind state.

Hormoany, basket in one hand, Parry's arm in the other, guided her charges towards the Great Hall. "You don't want to miss dinner," she said to Parry, who, on the whole, reasoned missing dinner was probably the least of his worries at the moment. "And anyway, familiar places will be good for him," she nodded to the basket.

They had a short trip along the corridor, then down a long flight of stairs to the main reception area, the Great Lobby, and through to the Great Hall. For once, the false perspective didn't bother Parry as he crossed the threshold, as he could barely see well enough to notice.

Hormoany was careful to guide Parry to the vicinity of a table, but as the food approached her change in priorities was quite noticeable. He found his way to a chair, half by touch and half by what remained of his vision, blurred in one eye, half burnt-out in the other.

All the while, Hormoany was chatting to Parry about her investigations. "Apparently," she said, compulsively filling her plate, "the wizard child with two fathers has been a theme in prophecy for at least the last three thousand years, possibly longer. The prophecy talks about power and control – DON'T SIT THERE!" Hormoany screamed a warning, preventing Parry from crushing Freddie. "Just put him on the floor if you want to sit there. Yes, that's better.

"Now apparently, the child with the two fathers holds within himself amazing power."

"I can't say I've noticed any amazing power," said Parry, blinking at the 'food' on the table in front of him.

"You can't eat that," said Hormoany.

"Why not?"

"Because they're my material swatches for the new play."

She took his hand and put it on a plate holding something bread-like. Actually, from Parry's point of view, it was probably a blessing that he couldn't quite see what he was eating.

But he could swear he heard sniggering again.

"The trouble is," said Hormoany, "it all refers to the Grimoire of the Sorcerer Awkinsh. Now, that's a very rare book, but I know from when my sister did her work that we've got a copy in the school. So I went to the library, but it was missing."

Parry pulled out the wing that was stuck in his teeth. Fortunately he never actually saw what it was.

"Anyway," said Hormoany, "I went along to see Samantha. You know, the girl I did the fagging for the other night. Well, she's a library trustee, and she asked Tabitha who asked Arleen, and *she* said her friend had been told they'd all been removed for safe keeping."

Parry was listening to the calls from the other side of the dining room. "Oi, Parry, is it true you've never heard of Mother's Day?"

"Hormoany – You haven't told anybody about this prophecy, have you?" Hormoany was so offended she sprayed a little food on the table as she spoke.

and the seamy side of magic

"No," she said indignantly. "I haven't *told* anybody. But obviously, I've *discussed it* with a few people…"

Another voice came from across the room. "Oi, Hotter, is it right your mum's got a willy?"

"I wonder," said Parry, largely to himself, "if that troll is still hungry."

"You!" cried a furious voice on the very edge of reason. "It's you!"

Jape was staggering down from the top table, one hand on his pained stomach, the other pointing accusingly at an oblivious Parry Hotter.

"What's going on?" asked Parry.

"I think," said Hormoany, gathering up two plates of food, "it's time to leave."

"You parasite of my being!"

Jape's fury whipped the air around him. Tornado-like, it was sucking up pieces of cutlery. A knife and fork collided in the whirlwind and ricocheted with lethal force; the knife embedding itself into the stone wall, the fork into an unfortunate child's shoulder blade.

"What's going on?" asked Parry.

"Follow me!" called Hormoany, from the doorway.

"You abomination!" cried Jape, advancing with heavy, pained footsteps. "You taunt me with your every breath!"

Miss Featherstone ran between them. "Now, Jape, I really don't see –" As she approached the whirlwind she was lifted from her feet and thrown skyward, creating a new hole in a recently repaired section of roof.

Jarvaris, the charms teacher, and the Bursar were the next to try to intervene.

"Hallo?" called Parry. "Jude, what's happening? Jude?"

Wands at the ready, the two wizards approached Jape.

They pointed their wands at each other, and muttered a spell, inaudible to all but themselves. A crackling line of power joined the two wands as the wizards walked towards Jape.

"Now, son," said Jarvaris as he and the Bursar's approached, "we don't want to hurt you, but we can't let you do anything silly now, can we?"

Jape's storm of fury touched the line. It held for very nearly a tenth of a second before the two wizards were violently flung away.

Jape, his storm now infused with a fiery blue glow, continued his advance.

"Hallo?" said Parry, plaintively. "Anybody there?"

"Because of you I've lived my life in shame!" cried Jape.

The Headmaster wiped his mouth. He didn't hold with nonsense, and any sort of carry-on which interrupted his mealtime – well, that was certainly nonsense.

"Because of you I've wasted away for so many years!" screamed Jape, dragging himself forward.

The Headmaster rounded the front of the table and looked about for something useful.

"Because of you my career was destroyed!" accused Jape.

After testing the sturdiness of a couple of chairs the Headmaster settled for a leg from the wizards great table, and wrenched it out of place. The table creaked and groaned as it adjusted to its missing support.

"*Because of you I have rotted in the backwaters of our society, ashamed to call myself by my own name.*" Jape's voice was no longer screaming. Now it was a much more menacing growl.

Bol d'Areth took a couple of practice swings with the table-leg.

"*I shall correct the mistake I had not the strength to correct at the time. In your death you will feel every moment of shame I have lived for fifteen long years.*"

"Hallo? Will someone please talk to me?"

"*Now die, instrument of my torture and humiliation!*"

Jape began the lethal spell. One word, two words – then his eyes bulged, his neck straightened, his arms went limp, and he fell to the floor.

"Fine piece of wood," Bol d'Areth congratulated himself. "Very good indeed." He relived the swing once or twice.

"Bursar, Bursar, where the devil are you, man?" Bol d'Areth spotted the Bursar propped against the wall. He found a jug of water and threw it, with surprising accuracy, considering the distance.

The Bursar coughed and spluttered. "When reviving the unconscious," he remarked, dragging himself to his feet, "it is usual to decant the water before throwing it, sir."

"Do I own a set of golf clubs?" Bol d'Areth asked, once more testing the air with the table leg.

"Er, no, sir," replied the Bursar, distressed that his ever-immaculate clothing had been disarranged and dampened.

"Ah," said Bol d'Areth. "Get me some, would you? There's a good chap. Oh, and do something about this mess."

The Bursar only nodded as he watched the collapse of the three-legged top table.

Gordon chose that moment to enter, showing a guest from Ogs-Warth School into the main room. "And this, of course, is the…"

He paused in mid-speech and surveyed the devastation, the collapsed top table, the trail of carnage through the centre of the room, the bleeding pupils and the prone wizards, not to mention the enormous toad that was helping itself to whatever had fallen to the floor.

"I think, perhaps," considered Gordon, "I'll rustle up some eggs Benedict at home."

CHAPTER 7

Understandably, neither Parry nor Freddie was at his best in the following morning's levitation lesson.

Parry was still trying to comprehend the information that Jape was his father, although Hormoany's insistence that Jape was actually his *mother* did nothing to brighten his mood, even once he had two hundred percent of his vision back. He had hoped that by this morning the double vision would have gone.

Of course the news that Jape was his – well, let's say parent, shall we? – was somewhat cushioned by the fact that Parry was convinced that Hormoany was on some kind of wind-up.

At their levitation class, Freddie was struggling even more than Parry. The most he'd been able to make his piece of chalk do was to shake and rattle on the desk. However, telling Freddie he wasn't any good because he was so spineless, left Parry winded for a minute and a half from the resulting body blow. At least Parry could get his chalk in the air, and spent a fair part of the lesson fetching it back from wherever it landed.

Hormoany, meanwhile, was practising writing her alphabet without touching the chalk.

At least the potions lesson which followed was relatively easy. Professor Simova, sitting in for the injured Miss Featherstone, concentrated on the techniques of mixing potions, rather than any specific magical outcome, so for Parry it served as an introduction to cooking.

※

Goodie Deux-Pantoufles had seen them coming the other way. He paused, but decided he'd keep going, anyway, head held high.

"Yeah, but it's clear," Parry was saying, "that Jape's insane, going around nursing his stomach all the time."

and the seamy side of magic

"He only does that when you're around," said Freddie.

"Yeah, but why would my dad…" – Hormoany raised an eyebrow – "No," said Parry. "I can't accept that."

The two boys slid their arms under Goodie's armpits and lifted him off the floor. "But if Jape's my parent," said Parry, choosing his words carefully, "Who is, well, you know, the other one?"

"Now that is a mystery," said Freddie, guiding them over to a functional door recessed into the corridor wall. "Who on earth would shag Jape?"

Their voices disappeared as they went down the service stairs.

At the top of the stairs Hormoany waited impatiently, tapping her foot and glancing at her wrist dial. She heard the muffled struggling.

But very soon the two boys were returning. "Of course, if we could find that prophecy Hormoany was yapping about, all things might be made clear."

"Really?" Parry was encouraged. "That would be really good."

"No, not really," said Freddie. "Prophecies are never straightforward. It's part of the whole prophecy deal – be a bit vague, be a bit unclear, lose a couple of pages here and there. I reckon half the prophets numbered their pages one, two, three, seven, just to give them an air of mystery and authenticity.

"You prophesy anything vaguely enough it's going to come true, nine times out of ten. All you need is half a dozen centuries, and a reader with a fertile imagination."

༺ঞ༻

"And of course, gentlemen, to round off your visit to the school, chef has prepared something very special indeed," announced the Bursar to the assembled Warthogs staff and visiting Ogs-Warth School dignitaries.

The enormous platter was laid on the table, and with a flourish the chef whipped off the domed cover. It was only the Bursar's lightning-fast reactions, parrying the Headmaster's long-pronged fork and carving knife with a candlestick from his end of the table, that saved Goodie from getting more than superficial puncture wounds.

"I say," said Smudge, "doesn't the apple usually go in the other end?"

The Bursar pulled the onion from the young man's mouth. "I think perhaps you had better explain, Mr Deux-Pantoufles?"

༻♡༺

"A month of detentions," complained Freddie.

"Yeah, it's beginning to feel like my old school already," grumbled Parry.

"Did you see it there?" asked Hormoany. "The Grimoire of Awkinsh?"

"Hard to say for sure," replied Freddie. "The Bursar was in the way of the cabinet most of the time, but several of the other titles you mentioned were there, so I'd say it's a safe bet."

Hormoany, Freddie and Parry toiled away, pulling down the more excessive growth of Gordon's vines.

"These lessons are bad enough. Did he have to give us detention with Gordon, too?"

"It's no more than you deserve," declared Hormoany.

Parry tugged hard at the climbers. They came away in a clump. "Oops!" he said.

"Children, children, children!" came Gordon's distinctive voice from behind them. "I told you, not *too* much."

Parry, Freddie and Hormoany were staring at the hand-shape they had uncovered, outlined against the wall by a black charring.

"You just can't paint over those things, and believe me, I've tried," complained Gordon. "Now let me see if I can find a hanging basket. We'll just have to put it up there until the larmagainvillaea grows back."

"This still means that we're going to have to send the roving eye to make sure," Freddie told Parry, "and we're going to have to practise our borrowing skills."

"Well, technically speaking, we'll have to *learn* some borrowing skills," said Parry.

"Easy," said Freddie. "It's our next lesson."

"Well, I hope you get on better than you did with Levitation and Transfiguration and History of Magic – and Kwadwaq, come to that," commented Hormoany.

The boys looked at one another, and then dumped half the climber on her head.

"Do try to be more careful!" called Gordon from behind them. "After all, we're going to be seeing *so* much more of each other."

※

Borrowing did turn out to be a frustrating lesson for Freddie and Parry alike. The tutor called himself Master Xang, but if there was anything Far Eastern in his inheritance, it must have been bone china teacups, handed down through the family.

Nevertheless, he persisted with an unnecessary squint, Chinese-style clothes and an accent out of a 1970s Kung Fu movie, despite the obvious disapproval of those in the class with genuine Far Eastern roots, or whatever parallel that culture had in this world.

The bench in front of Freddie showed a number of dents, testifying to his frustration with his inability to master the spell. Freddie's designated cork on the long bench at the front of the lecture hall had done little more than shake and swivel. Parry's cork lay on the floor between the front desk and his own, and refused to approach closer, despite or possibly due to the fact that now he was interjecting between the magic words the intensifiers 'bloody', 'stupid', 'effing' and 'thing'.

"Ah," said Xang, "I see here there is need of my tuition. I must teach you to empty your mind, to be one with the cork. Let the magical incantation flow through your body. Allow me to demonstrate."

He closed his eyes, breathing deeply from his diaphragm he took a few moments to centre himself. Bringing his arms up over his head, he pressed his palms together as he brought his hands down past his face and his chest. Reaching out he held open one hand and mumbled the magic words.

"*Etgay vero erehum ownum row lsee.*"

The cork raised itself lazily from the far bench, meandered across to the pseudo Far Eastern master, bobbing just a little way off the floor, until reaching his feet, and hopping up into his hand. "Now, once more, you try it."

"Oh, I'm sorry, were you talking to me?" Hormoany woke up from her copy of '*The Magical Times*'. She raised her hands, and her lips barely moved as she mumbled the spell. Her cork flew from its resting-place on the front desk and hit her hand with an audible slap.

Forgetting himself, Xang's eyes momentarily widened.

Xang stared at her Hormoany for a moment. "In your own time, boys," he said, and left them to it.

Parry and Freddie glanced at one another. Parry moved his head close to Hormoany's, although she continued reading the newspaper as if oblivious.

"Judicita," Parry whispered, "have I told you how much I admire and respect you?"

"Yeah, yeah," said Hormoany. "I'll help steal the books for you. You'd just better make it worth my while."

ଚ∞ଚ

Hormoany had an early dinner, and was halfway through the generous supplies she'd brought back to the room for the boys by the time they'd finished their detention with Gordon.

"I can't believe how much my hand hurts," grumbled Parry, cradling his right hand in his left.

Freddie was painfully flexing his own hands. "I must admit, that wasn't easy."

"What did he have you do?" asked Hormoany, fascinated.

"Cutting the grass," Parry told her.

Hormoany looked between their faces and their hands for a couple of moments. "Are you going to make me ask again?" she demanded.

and the seamy side of magic 139

Parry cottoned on. "No, we've been using wire cutters. Patch of needlegrass, or something, had sprung up on the Kwadwaq field, and a couple more tufts towards the pavilion."

"Never seen any so tough," said Freddie.

"We've still got time," said Hormoany, glancing at her wrist-dial. "They've got those people from Ogs-Warth School of Witchcraft over, so we've probably got another two courses before many of the wizards will be out. I expect most of them will retire for drinks anyway."

"Well, let's get on with it," said Parry, handing the eyeball to Freddie. Freddie pronounced the magic words, and held the eyeball out of the window. Released, it flew off around the building.

"How's it going to get into the Headmaster's office?" Parry wondered.

"Easy," said Freddie. "These buildings are old. There are gaps in the eaves, ventilation spaces under the floors – there are a million and one little cracks and gaps in a building like this. A roving eye like that is programmed to find the most effective entrance route."

They turned their attention to the crystal ball which showed a dimly lit window, approaching at speed. The image jolted, then the view was a stationary one, the eye hovering inside the office.

Parry and Freddie looked at one another. "*Neo undredhay ae ightyea,*" command Freddie.

The image swivelled around. They could see the hole the roving eye had punched in the window.

"Of course," said Freddie, "it's always a good idea to engage stealth mode, if you remember in time."

"Hurry up and look for the book," urged Hormoany. "We may have set off an alarm of some kind."

Freddie repeated the command, but Hormoany cried a warning as their view of the room swivelled around. "Look! The door handle is moving!"

"*Ngagee ealthsti odem!*" Freddie called just in time.

The eyeball raised suddenly to ceiling height, and hovered in a corner. The door opened slowly and a figure slipped inside, pausing only to look up and down the corridor before gently closing the door.

"Jape," said Hormoany.

"Do you think he's there because of the window?" asked Parry.

"No," said Freddie, "he hasn't even looked at it. He's gone over to the book cabinet."

They saw Jape take out his wand and tap the four hinges of the bookcase. The key turned itself in the lock, and the doors opened. He ran his finger across the hide-bound volumes till he found the one he was looking for, and hefted it out of its place.

"That's it, that's it!" cried Hormoany. "That's the Grimoire of the Sorcerer Awkinsh! He's stealing our book before we've even had a chance to nick it ourselves!"

"Quick!" said Parry. "Get the eyeball to follow Jape. We need to know where he hides the book."

"Yeah, yeah," said Freddie. "Way ahead of you." He leafed through the roving eye's instruction manual.

※

Jape took a slender volume from the bottom shelf of the cabinet, and slipped it in the place of the heavy book. He tapped it twice with his wand, and it became an apparent reproduction of the Grimoire of the Sorcerer Awkinsh. Satisfied with the likeness, the wizard slipped the original book beneath his cloak.

Jape tapped his wand on the cabinet again. The doors closed, the lock turned. He crept to the office door, opened it a crack, glancing up and down the corridor before stepping out. The roving eye slipped out through the door behind him, and hovered unseen back toward the ceiling.

Jape pulled the door to, and tapped it with his wand. He heard the lock click back into place.

"This way! Hurry now!" came the voice of the Bursar. Jape could hear them on the stairs. He looked around for one urgent moment, then he moved apart two urns on the windowsill. He placed the book between them, and with a little shimmer the book was another decorative urn.

and the seamy side of magic

"Jape, what are you doing here?" snapped the Bursar.

"Don't be impertinent, man!" returned Jape. "My office is only down the hall."

"Of course. I'm sorry, but one cannot be too careful."

He pointed his wand at Jape, and zigzagged it over his body. Jape's robes billowed, as if blown by a powerful jet of air. Angrily, Jape gestured with his hand, and the Bursar's wand was knocked aside – but the search was already complete. "As I said," continued the Bursar, "one can never be too careful. The Headmaster's room has been interfered with."

"How?" started Jape. "I mean, who?"

"That we must see. Places in the corridor, gentlemen," the Bursar said to the two wizards accompanying him. "Let us see who dares insult Bol d'Areth!"

The Bursar inserted a key into the lock, and, pushing the door open, gestured with his free hand. The lights in the room immediately burnt brightly. "The window," he said, "see?" pointing at the hole. He moved across to inspect it, and looked down and saw the glass on the carpet.

Moving anticlockwise around the room he checked the cabinets, first the cabinet with the books, and then the others.

"Everything appears secure," the Bursar conceded. "Perhaps the intruder was alerted to our alarm when he broke the window."

"If it *were* an intruder," said Jape. "Might that not have been a stone or a bat? They're known to hunt moths on windows, you know."

"On them," said the Bursar. "Very rarely through them. And I see no stone."

"A wand blast, perhaps?" suggested Jape.

"No doubt. Probably some fifth years getting trigger-happy with their new wands. I'm sure boiled cabbage for their dinner tomorrow and an explanation as to why will cool off the hotter heads.

"Thank you for your time, Jape," said the Bursar pointedly. "I know you've not been very…" he deliberated a moment upon the right word – "well. Don't allow me to detain you any further on this matter."

Jape nodded. It was clear that the courtesy in both men was only paper-thin.

As the door shut behind Jape the Bursar strode to the book cabinet, tapping its four hinges. The door sprung open. He grabbed the Grimoire of the Sorcerer Awkinsh. Laying it on the table he carefully opened it.

"Ubarbrh," the Bursar read, "ubarbrh, ubarbrh, ubarbrh," then punched the worthless pages. "Curses!" he swore, and glared at the doorway through which Jape had disappeared.

※

"Jape's gone," said Parry.

"He's left the urn," pointed out Hormoany.

"Must be waiting until the coast's clear," reckoned Freddie. "I expect the Bursar must be suspicious. He'll want to come back for it when the heat has died down a little."

"I'm sorry, but I'm bursting," said Hormoany, excusing herself. "Don't let anything exciting happen while I'm gone."

"We've got to get that urn before Jape comes back for it," said Freddie.

"Damn right," agreed Parry. "Let's go."

Freddie led the way, calling back over his shoulder, "And bring the crystal ball. We'll need it." With a hint of resignation Parry lifted the heavy globe and followed Freddie.

Barely a minute or so later Hormoany dashed back into the room, still drying her hands on her dress. "Right, what I think we – oh, blast them!"

※

Much of the building, busy by day, was deathly quiet in the evening. Nevertheless, the boys felt safer crouching in a dimly lit classroom off the main corridor while they watched the images in the crystal ball. The roving eye had gone up and down the corridor twice now, the only living soul it had seen was Goodie Deux-Pantoufles, no doubt on some errand for the greater good.

and the seamy side of magic

"Okay," said Freddie. "I've sent it to watch the stairs. Right," he nodded toward an intersection a short distance up the passage, "take that junction, turning right at a run, and you'll be in the top corridor."

For Parry, who had experienced a number of the school's charmed shortcuts when chased by the ghoul, it made a pleasant change to know where he might end up. Freddie took the crystal ball off him. "Off you go then. Make it quick. If I see anyone coming I'll knock the roving eye on the ceiling three times."

Parry opened his mouth to complain about being volunteered as the thief, but realized it would be futile. Anybody would think it was Freddie's crystal ball, but he had learned the command words which, Parry would have to admit, was more than he had done himself.

With a last glance into the crystal ball, and a final check to make sure the coast was clear, Parry set off at a run. Almost instantly he was in the top corridor. He decelerated as rapidly as he could, trying to avoid making too much noise. He jogged along until he was outside the Headmaster's office.

He looked at the urns. He picked one up. He thought he remembered where Jape had put it, but it's always difficult to say when you're looking through the fishbowl distortions of the crystal ball. 'Right,' he thought, and ran back down the corridor.

He was suddenly back in the lower corridor. He nipped into the classroom where Freddie was waiting. "Is this it?"

"I don't know," said Freddie. "You were the one going to get it."

"Well, do you think it *might* be it?" asked Parry, hopefully.

Freddie turned the urn around in his hands. "Difficult to say, really. We're probably looking for one that's a bit different."

"Is that one different?" asked Parry.

Freddie looked at him. "Different from what?"

Parry sighed, and made another dash for the junction.

A minute or two later the boys were comparing two urns.

"Is one different?" Parry was asking Freddie.

"Well," said Freddie, "this one's different from that one."

"Then that's the one!" said Parry.

"And that one," said Freddie, "is different from this one."

"So that could be the one," said Parry. "So which one is the different one?"

"Well, they're both different from each other," said Freddie.

"Ah," said Parry, seeing the flaw in their logic. "Back in a minute."

They'd forgotten their previous caution. Now they had three urns lined up in a row on the master's desk.

"So what we're saying is this," recapped Parry. "This one is different from this one and this one, this one in the middle is different from the two at the ends, and the one on this end is different from the one in the middle and the one on that end."

"Right!" said Freddie.

"And we're looking for one that's different."

"Yep," agreed Freddie.

"But they're all different."

"Mm," said Freddie. "Tricky."

∞

It is an unvarying natural law that when one is trying to be quiet one makes more noise than ever would be possible without the effort of trying to make no noise at all. When one is laden with two bed sheets full of clay urns the noise has a tendency to reach a crescendo rarely heard outside a trendy nightclub or demolition site.

Parry and Freddie came crashing and clunking noisily through their dorm door.

"Where the hell have *you* been?" demanded Hormoany.

"*Shhh!*" hushed Freddie, redundantly.

"We went to get the urn, only we weren't quite sure..." said Parry, dragging his cargo in and letting the door slam shut behind him.

"...exactly which one it was," finished Freddie.

"You *are* ridiculous," said Hormoany, presenting an urn in front of them. "I borrowed it, the minute I got back. I've been sitting here on my own for two hours, wondering where the hell you were, and I'm starving!"

"So," wondered Parry aloud, "what are we going to do with all these urns?" The boys looked at each other and then to Hormoany, expectantly.

"Don't look at *me*," she said. "It's called 'borrowing', not 'returning'."

CHAPTER 8

"Shh! I'm trying to listen," hushed Hormoany, impatiently.

"Pardon me for breathing," replied Parry.

"They rarely do, you know," said Freddie, filling his second breakfast bowl. For once Hormoany was so distracted he had even got a little ahead of her in the consumption stakes.

"Quiet," she said. "I can't hear what they're saying."

"Well, what are they saying that is so interesting?" asked Parry.

Freddie put on a silly voice. "Oooh, do you like the new material for my flying robe? Oh, and have you heard about my cousin's sister's friend's new cat?"

"Quiet!" snapped Hormoany. "I'm missing all the good stuff!"

"How can you hear anything?" asked Parry. "They're sitting two tables away."

"I can't hear anything while you're going on in my ear, now can I?"

"Is it like some super hearing spell?" wondered Parry.

"It's like a super shut-up spell in a minute!" warned Hormoany.

"Oooh," it was Parry's turn for a silly voice. "Get her."

Barely looking round, Hormoany's wand came up and tapped Parry's chair. Parry hit the floor in a cloud of sawdust.

One of the girls Hormoany was listening to stood up. She was wiping back a tear that had escaped the corner of her eye. "If that's how you feel about it!" She snatched a card out of the other girl's hand and tore it up, throwing it back at her.

"Honestly, I don't understand!" the second girl protested, and was then chasing the first girl out of the hall.

"There, look. See!" accused Hormoany. "You made me miss the best bit."

"What's the big deal?" Parry dragged a new chair over.

"Well, Delia and Yasbeth are on the committee, if you know what I mean."

"What committee?" asked Parry, who clearly had no idea what she meant.

"You know, the women's committee."

"You like all that organizing stuff," said Freddie. "Why aren't you on the committee?"

"Believe me, if every boy in this place was like you I would be. Anyway, Delia gave Yasbeth a card to thank her for – you know – a romantic evening last night?"

"Oh," the penny finally dropped with Parry. "You mean…"

"Anyway," continued Hormoany, "Yasbeth asked Delia what she meant. Delia got all upset and embarrassed and angry at Yasbeth, and Yasbeth kept asking what the hell was going on."

"Riveting," said Freddie.

"You sure you're over the whole toad thing?" asked Parry.

"Well, it's the talk of the ladies' powder room," said Hormoany. "You see, they're not the only ones. On Tuesday Abigail and Gabriel had the same sort of row. On Wednesday it was Catherine and Avedum, on Thursday it was Kira and Pynchon. Now today it's those two!"

"Fascinating," said Freddie dryly.

"And you've overheard all this sitting there?" asked Parry.

"Don't be silly. We all saw Catherine and Avedum, and Jessica told me about Kira and Pynchon, and Zelda told me about Abigail and Gabriel, because she heard it from Tanita."

"Right from the horse's mouth," said Freddie.

"Do you mean what you're supposed to mean?" demanded Hormoany. "Or are you being rude about Tanita?"

There was a flapping sound and something slapped onto Hormoany's head. "Ah," said Freddie. "Saved by the bat!"

Parry had seen the bats deliver post of a morning, and a number being sent out with letters in the evening. Apparently the bats generally preferred to travel overnight. Which sort of made sense, if you thought about it.

But this was the first time Parry had seen a delivery up close. Hormoany plucked a moth out of the insect bread to entice the bat off her head, and allow her to detach the small scroll from the creature's harness, dropping a small coin from her considerable purse in its place.

The bat seemed content with this, and releasing the last strands of her hair happily went to inspect the insect bread to see if there was anything more he could enjoy. "Oh, it's from mother," said Hormoany. "She just wondered how well I'm settling in. Isn't that nice?"

Parry held his bowl off the table, ready to leap backwards at the first sign that the bat was interested in him.

Freddie looked at Hormoany's letter, at the bat ambling down the table, and at Parry. Heavy cogs turned over inside his mind.

"Oh I nearly forgot," said Hormoany with feigned casualness, "I've got something for you Parry." She folded up the letter into her bag and produced a phial of clear liquid. "Its best to have it on a full stomach."

"What is it?" Parry shook the tiny bottle suspiciously.

"Oh it's a, it's a protection charm. I thought, in the circumstances…"

"A charm in a bottle?" asked Freddie sceptically.

"It took me ages to get the ingredients and to get the incantations right. Come on, you've got to down it in one."

"It smells like vodka."

"Is that a good thing?"

"I suppose so." Blackmailed by Hormoany's expectant gaze, Parry threw her concoction down his throat. "*Hewereezzzeah!*"

Hormoany grabbed Parry's face and forced him to look right at her. "This is very important Parry. How do you feel?"

"*Sick*," Parry rasped.

"Love sick?" Hormoany prompted.

"No, just physically sick," said Parry, regaining his ability to speak. "And this'll keep me safe, will it?"

"Yeah, right. Whatever." A clearly disappointed Hormoany released Parry's face.

Parry caught Freddie's amused eye and found himself unable to tear his gaze away from his friend. "Have I ever told you what a terribly attractive man you are, Freddie?"

"You what?"

"Oh hell!" swore a frustrated Hormoany, fetching a vicious looking needle and syringe from her bag. "Hold him still Freddie, I've got to administer the antidote intravenously..."

※

The only thing that kept Parry going through the morning's lessons was the knowledge that, this being Friday, he had the afternoon off.

As Parry understood it, this was the beginning of the weekend, and this afternoon Hormoany was going to have another crack at changing the urn back into a book.

She knew one or two rectification spells, but they weren't nearly powerful enough. Although they could change back an object she herself had changed, they hadn't dented the morphic field Jape had used on the book. He was, after all, the Transfiguration Master.

If he changed something, he was intending it to stay that way until he himself changed it back. But Hormoany did have a lot of books, a number handed down from her sister, and many vacuumed from the school library before any other interested parties got a look in.

Hormoany was going to see what she could find this afternoon, and see if she could undo Jape's magic. This made the Bursar's rendition of Metaphysics, The Theory of Magic, seem even longer than it would otherwise have done. Some people theorized that he actually slowed the passage of time to get four full boring lecture hours into the two that his lesson was allotted.

The second lesson was not much of a relief, either. It was called Predictive Science. Last year it had been called Futurology, the year before that, Seeing, the year before that, Reading Signs and Entrails.

Almost the whole of the Predictive Science lesson was taken up with the teacher, Wish-Moon the Elder, complaining about the crisis in astrology as the mortals kept finding one new celestial body after another, and the rival theories in astrology about whether the predictions should be adjusted for the new information, or whether the bias the unseen bodies had been influencing was already built in to the body of predictive lore.

But Freddie did at least encourage Parry to stay awake with the warming news that the lessons did get better later in the term, when they got round to reading the decanted contents of chickens, goats and the like.

Parry said he couldn't wait, first with irony, but then with conviction. Chickens and even goats, he remembered, were at least edible.

As soon as they had finished the Predictive Science lesson Parry and Freddie dashed back to their room to await Hormoany who had Double Sympathetic Magic on Friday morning, so they could have another crack at undoing the spell on the book.

They'd probably waited about twenty minutes before realizing that Hormoany would have headed straight for the Great Hall and lunch first. They thought they'd better go and find her.

"Freddie," Parry called from the doorway.

"Yeah?"

"Did you have any problem getting out of the room?"

Freddie clearly thought this something of an odd question. "No, I can't say that I did, as evidenced by the fact that I'm in the corridor, and not in the aforementioned room."

"It's just," said Parry, "I don't seem to be able to…" He pushed against the unseen barrier in the doorway. It felt to him quite solid.

"Ah," said Freddie, "you've got – '*Imem ni ay Assgly Oxbium*'. Thresholditis, in lay terms."

"Do what?"

"Catches some of the newbies every year it does, but you'll be pleased to know it's not serious," Freddie reassured.

"Not serious!" echoed Parry. "I'm trapped in the room, and *you* think it's not serious."

"Well, it's only an allergy," said Freddie. "You become sensitive to the thresholds. It's not uncommon when people are moved to a magical environment. It just lasts a day or two, then it gets better by itself. Although I must say it's more common in children than teenagers."

"Oh, great! I've got the magical equivalent of chickenpox, just in time for the weekend! If I had to get it I could have at least got it when it would have done some good and got me out of a few lessons."

"Well, you're lucky you got it in your own room," said Freddie. "Many kids have to spend a couple of days in a street or a garden, and some of the first years here have spent a couple of nights sleeping in the corridors, or worse still, stuck in one of the teaching rooms, with someone like the Bursar or Smudge lecturing at them all day. No, if you're going to have this problem, now's the time to get it."

Hormoany arrived. "There you are," she said to them, as if they were the ones that had been lost. "I thought you might forget about lunch, so..." she manoeuvred a heavily laden tray through the doorway.

"Parry's got thresholditis," Freddie told her, following the food back into the room. "He's stuck in here."

"Oh," Hormoany was clearly disappointed. "I knew we should have done this in my room."

"That wouldn't have helped," said Freddie. "He would simply have been stuck in your room for a couple of days."

Hormoany made a point of not catching Freddie's eye. "Still," she said, "I've brought plenty of food. Honestly, how do you boys live in this mess? Can you make some room for me to sit down?"

She kicked her way through the loose objects on the floor – clothing, books and the like – until she reached the bed and, as nobody else seemed to want to do it, she grabbed an armful of stuff off one of the beds, stuck it down between the bed and the wardrobe, and sat down.

"Now," she said, as the boys helped themselves to a couple of sandwiches, "where's the urn?"

"I think you just kicked it under my bed," answered Freddie through a mouthful of lunch.

"Oh, honestly!" berated Hormoany, retrieving the urn. "This is a very important work of magical literature. You don't just leave it around the floor to get stood on and kicked about."

Freddie shrugged and helped himself to another sandwich. Hormoany inspected the urn for damage, and, having brushed off a couple of scrape marks, looked for somewhere to set it down.

Finding nowhere immediately suitable, she shoved several bits and pieces off the top of a bedside cabinet and stood the urn on there.

"*Estorer hetum dioti's pells* didn't do anything last night," said Hormoany, leafing through one of the larger books she'd brought with her. "Oh, yes, let's try this one."

Taking out her wand she tried, "*Sa nceoe ouy erewum, ebi os gainay*." The discharge from her wand shook the urn a little. It hummed and vibrated for a few moments, and then settled down.

"Perhaps if we both try," suggested Freddie, raising his wand. "On the count of three. One, two, three! – *Sa nceoe ouy erewum, ebi os gainay*."

"Well," said Hormoany. "You were supposed to be aiming at the urn. It's a good job I'm wearing sensible underwear."

Freddie sniggered.

With her wand Hormoany touched the yarn laying around her, and said; "*Estorer hetum dioti's pells*."

The yarn was once again her dress, and with a dirty look at the smirking Freddie she pulled it on over her head.

Hormoany continued leafing through the book. She kicked her feet, which were entwined in a top and some underwear. "Honestly! Ah, here's another one. Let's try this."

She pulled out her wand, "*Astcim waya oury isguisedus*." The urn made a kind of pinging noise.

"There's a sort of papery lining to it," remarked Freddie, leaning over the urn to inspect it.

"Hmm," said Hormoany, not very pleased with the slight change. "Don't crowd me," she said, manoeuvring one book down on the bed opposite, and pulling up another of her books from the floor. To be comfortable, she sat herself sideways on the bed.

"I don't know how you boys live in here. Not only do you keep it like a pigsty, it's so cramped!" she complained, putting her feet up on the other bed. *"Evealrium oury uetray acefay,"* Hormoany ordered, pointing her wand once more at the urn.

The texture of the urn clearly changed to something somewhat smoother. Hormoany tutted and picked up a third book. She leafed through it. "I might try this one – *oti ineth wnoum elfsum ebi uetray.*" This caused a flash when she cast the spell at the urn.

"Well, we now appear to have a leather-bound paper-lined urn," observed Freddie.

"Let me try as well," said Parry, picking up his wand. "The book is about me, after all."

"Well, you're mentioned in it," corrected Hormoany.

"Close enough," said Parry. "On three – one, two, three. *Oti ineth wnoum elfsum ebi uetray.*"

One half of Hormoany's chest suddenly deflated. "Will you watch where you're pointing your wand!" she shouted angrily.

Turning away from the boys she pointed her wand at herself and muttered, *"Amelap-n-dersona."* Restored, she turned back. "If you're not going to take this seriously, I'm not helping."

"What?" said Parry innocently.

"Much as I like a good fight," interrupted Freddie, "has anyone noticed how cramped it is in here?"

"Well," started Hormoany, "if just for once you'd tidy up…"

"No," said Freddie, "it's not exactly what I mean. For example, didn't there used to be some space to walk up and down between the beds?"

As if to underline his point the wooden frames of the beds started creaking as they pushed together.

"I think," said Freddie, "this might be a rather good time to leave."

"What about me?" asked Parry, nervously. "I'm stuck in this room!"

"Unfortunate, that," sympathised Freddie.

"Don't worry, Parry," said Hormoany earnestly. "We'll get help."

Parry was trying the window, unsuccessfully. "Well, I would appreciate it."

There was a snapping sound as the bed frames began to give way.

"Everyone out who's going out!" called Freddie, forcing open the room's door against the wardrobe that was now crowding it.

"I'll be back," promised Hormoany. "You can count on me."

She dashed to the door, and bounced off an invisible barrier. "You're not telling me I've got thresholditis!" she said angrily.

Freddie tried pushing at the space in the doorway. "No," he said, "I think it might be a tad more serious than that."

"What?" said Parry. "No one can get out?"

There came another snapping sound as wood gave way under compression.

"Help! Help!" cried Hormoany. The boys, who could pick up on basic ideas, added their voices.

"Help! Help!" the three cried. "We're stuck in this room, and it's shrinking!"

A number of people walked past in the corridor without even glancing their way. "Do you think they can hear us?" asked Freddie.

"I don't know," replied Hormoany. "You two, look out of that window. Don't turn round until I say."

"What are you doing?" asked Parry.

"I mean it," she said. "Just look out of that window."

Climbing over the broken bed frames, the boys did as they were told.

"We haven't got all day here," said Freddie. "Do you mind telling us what you're up to?"

"It's okay, you can turn round again now," Hormoany told the two boys, pulling her dress back on over her head. "They definitely can't see us, either."

There was a scraping sound as the wardrobes edged in towards one another. Hormoany made use of the little remaining gap to get on to the debris of the beds before the passageway closed up completely.

Parry saw something move under the debris, clothing and other detritus on the floor. "Something's in here!" he cried,

and the seamy side of magic

trying to climb to the highest point on the broken wood and mattresses. "There's something under there!"

"Leave off," said Freddie. "The rat's mine. You just eat the sandwiches if you're hungry."

The two wardrobes had met and were now creaking as the walls of the room inched ever further in.

"I don't think," Freddie grunted, braced between the two walls, "that I'm going to be able to stop these coming in."

Hormoany was using what space she had to leaf through the magic books. "Come on, come on!" she was saying to herself.

"Hurry up," pleaded Parry.

"This would be a lot easier," Hormoany said, "if the index wasn't in the old tongue."

"I don't think," Parry said, as the wardrobes exploded into splintered panelling, "that I've got the time to learn the language and help you."

"There's got to be something we can do," insisted Hormoany, searching the book index. "Of course! Transfiguration!"

"Oh great," said Parry. "I'm going to spend my last moments being crushed to death as a toad."

"If you're going to have a brilliant idea," said Freddie, his back against one wall, his feet against the other, his knees now pressing in towards his chest, "I think you'd better have it quick."

"We're going to prop the walls," said Hormoany. "I just need to figure out what the densest object in the room is."

༄

The darkness faded to grey, then the grey gave way to colour as his sight returned. He blinked slowly, almost mechanically at first. Something was wrong, uncomfortable. Then he realized what it was. With a groan Freddie allowed his legs to straighten and fall back onto the bed. He sucked in air for the first time in hours.

"Oh, thanks," said Freddie to Hormoany's anxious face as it peeped around Mr Tollopoff. "The densest object in the room…?"

"Well," she said, defensively, "you *were*. Anyway, you're part mountain troll. Being turned to stone must be like getting closer to your ancestors."

"It's not," Freddie said stiffly, "at all the same."

"Don't knock it," said Parry. "After all, it worked."

"Oh, it's good to have you back with us again," said Tollopoff brightly. "I've got very good news for you."

"I'm going to be okay?" asked Freddie.

"Better than that," said the tree surgeon. "Your furniture is going to be as good as new. I was able to save quite a lot of the frames. You don't get well-seasoned timber like that every day of the week. Antique, you know. The panelling on the wardrobes was splintered mind, perhaps I can make one decent out of what's left; but the beds – quality pieces of furniture – failed at their joints. As good as new in no time."

"We were very lucky Gordon and Jape got to us when they did," said Hormoany. "Gordon's vines had started shaking an alarm or something, so he knew something was up. It was a good job he didn't leave it much longer. You were starting to crack, you know."

"Gee, thanks," said Freddie. "That'll explain the pain then, will it?"

"I'll get some linseed oil," said the tree surgeon. "Great for loosening you up again, make you more supple."

Gordon and the Bursar came into Freddie's field of vision. "No need to thank me all at once," said Gordon.

"Certainly," said the Bursar, "it was very fortunate for the apprentices that you were aware of what was happening."

"Well, I do grow the larmagainvillaea for warning of just such an occurrence, but by the time I'd checked the perimeter I was lucky to find them in time."

"Indeed," commented the Bursar.

"I don't know what I might have done," said Gordon, "had Jape not been there to arrest the walls as I rescued the children."

"Young adults," corrected Hormoany.

"How very fortunate that Jape was in the vicinity, particularly as his feelings toward a certain young man are well known," said the Bursar, looking at Parry.

and the seamy side of magic

"Do you think he was – but then again," the Bursar changed track, "the Weasel family have been involved in many more than their fair share of, shall we say, *unfortunate* incidents; and it wouldn't be the first time one family member had fallen foul of another, would it, Frederick?"

"Hannibal and Damian always said that was an accident, sir," defended Freddie, trying to turn his head.

"Of course they did," said the Bursar.

"Right, now!" said the tree surgeon, returning with a pot and a brush. "I think we'd better give the patient some privacy," he said, loading the brush with the linseed oil. "Unless, of course," a thought appeared to have struck him, "you'd prefer mineral oil?"

Freddie simply groaned.

๛

Had the burning lamp been anything but magical, it would have extinguished some hours ago. Red dust lay around the floor of the office, and covered the desk.

A thin hand reached down for perhaps the one-hundredth time that evening. Using all his remaining self-control he pushed aside a pile of dust from the middle of the table, heaping it with the rest, and placed the last of the urns in the centre.

He took two or three deep breaths to try to steady himself. Magic worked best when you were in a calm frame of mind. His wand touched the urn.

"Everser hetum oncealerck's rtificea!"

For perhaps the one hundredth time that night he watched a clay urn explode into dust. He finally allowed himself the luxury of losing his temper. His fists hammered the table, sending a great cloud of red dust into the air.

"Uckfay!" Jape swore. "Uckfay, uckfay, uckfay!"

CHAPTER 9

Freddie, who had remained fairly uncommunicative all Friday evening – boiled cabbage for dinner didn't exactly help – brightened up a lot on Saturday morning. To an extent this was due to the letter he had received from his gran.

Admittedly, it was replying to a letter he had sent her some time last year but, as Freddie freely admitted, his gran wasn't as quick off the mark as she used to be. He was also pleased with himself for having had the idea to go to his brothers to purchase a rectification spell, to turn their leather-bound, paper-lined urn back into a book.

"Don't you think it's the least bit suspicious," demanded Hormoany, as they hurried back to her room, "that they just happened to have a first class rectification spell on the tips of their tongues, just when we happened to need it?"

"Well, you know me bros," said Freddie. "They're always handling all kinds of..." he searched for the right word.

"Stolen?" suggested Hormoany

"...discreet goods," finished Freddie. "They're probably doing that kind of thing all the time."

"And what, exactly, is a chattel?" she asked.

"Don't worry, Jude," reassured Freddie. "They can't enforce that clause until you're eighteen."

They reached Hormoany's room. She unlocked the door and Freddie, at least, followed her in. Her room was somewhat larger than the boys', even before their recent misadventure.

The boys' room had space only for the two wardrobes, one either side of the door, then further up the two beds lay with their heads to the window and their feet to the door, with only the minimum passageway between them.

Hormoany's room, however, was palatial in comparison. There were two beds, whose heads were against the right-hand wall, and their feet were at least four or five paces from the opposite wall.

There was plenty of room for shelves, for cupboards, for drawers, for vanity units and even a desk and chair. To add insult to injury, Hormoany and her roommate shared an en-suite bathroom.

"At least if the walls start coming in here," observed Parry, casting a jealous eye over the size of the room, "we'll have most of the day to worry about getting out again."

Hormoany tutted, and busied herself recovering the urn from its hiding-place in her trunk on top of the wardrobe. She unwrapped the towels that were keeping the urn safe, and set it down on the desk.

"Come in and shut the door," she told Parry.

"If it's all the same to you I think I'm more comfortable here," he said from his vantage point in the doorway.

"It's not all the same to me," said Hormoany. "What if someone sees what we're doing? It's not like they're going to try the same trick again. All the school staff will be prepared for that kind of trouble, and I've put some protection spells on the room myself. Now, come on."

Dubiously, Parry conceded. Locking the door behind him he joined Freddie and Hormoany.

"Now," Hormoany flourished her wand, "let's just see how good this magic is." She tapped the wand on the urn, "*Everser hetum oncealerck's rtificea!*"

The urn vibrated and jolted. A rectangular bulge appeared low down on the urn.

"It's working!" said Parry. "Have another go!"

Hormoany repeated the words, and this time the shape of the book was fully formed, with a heavy urn motif on the top. The third time she said the magic words the book appeared fully formed.

"Excellent!" said Parry, snatching up the book. "Now for some answers."

"Oi!" objected Hormoany. "I changed it back. You should let me read it first."

"Ah," agreed Parry. "I think that might be a good idea." He handed the book to Hormoany. "It's written in complete gibberish."

Hormoany looked at the page, then back at Parry. She turned the book the right way up and said, "It's not gibberish. It's just the ancient tongue."

"Can you read it?" asked Freddie over her shoulder.

"Well, this bit says '*Otof ne Urciam*'."

"And what does *that* mean?" asked Parry.

"Is it important?" wondered Freddie.

"Printed in Murcia," translated Hormoany, deflating the boys' expectations.

"Right, I'm going to need my Ancient Languages dictionary," she said, pointing to a large tome at the end of one of her bookcases, "and a *very* large bag of blood doughnuts."

༺༻

"So, to summarize," said Parry, "the nectar of power is contained in" – he searched for the appropriate words – "the unholy fruit of the usurper of the mother goddess, and I'm the…"

"Fruit. Yes."

"Could we use the term 'offspring'?"

Hormoany considered this. "Yes, we could, but it says 'fruit'."

"Okay," said Parry, "and the usurper of the mother goddess is…"

"Your mum, or at least, one of your dads."

"So I've got two dads and one mum."

"No," corrected Hormoany, "not really. You've got one sire and one usurper."

"Yeah," said Parry. "Not helping."

"Well, your sire is your real father as such," said Hormoany, consulting notes on the backs of several of the discarded Mystic Pizza boxes.

"And the usurper is?" asked Parry.

"The thing that took the place of your mother's womb."

and the seamy side of magic 161

"What?" said Freddie. "His dad did it with a cow or a sheep or something?"

"No," said Hormoany, genuinely disgusted. "Or at least, I don't think so. The usurper has replaced the female goddess, so I don't think we're talking wombs here. Or, well, not natural ones."

"What, you think he was hatched from an egg?" asked Freddie.

Parry glared at him.

"What?" said Freddie. "Trolls are hatched from eggs – some of them, anyway."

"No," said Hormoany again, "we've got this whole two fathers thing. One of them must have usurped the mother god. Eggs aren't mentioned anywhere."

"Yeah," said Freddie. "They probably wouldn't be mentioned just like, straight out. They'd probably call them 'The Great Orbs, nice with toast if boiled for three minutes', or something."

Hormoany tried to ignore Freddie. "Of course, it could have been done by magic. These are wizards we're talking about. It's going to have to have been magic of some kind."

"And this 'nectar of power' flowing through me?"

"Blood," said Hormoany.

"That makes me, like, really powerful, does it?" asked Parry, hopefully.

"Erm," considered Hormoany. "No."

"Figures," said Parry.

"But it will make your sire, well, according to this, *'first amongst wizards, for only within him shall the power endure'*."

"I see," said Parry, "and just how is my blood supposed to do that? You what, use a little drop in a potion, or dab a little on his forehead, or…"

"He drinks it," said Hormoany.

"A little?" asked Parry. "Are we talking a little taste here?"

"No," said Hormoany. "I think we're talking job lot."

"Ah," said Parry. "So he won't actually be able to become all-powerful…"

"Unless he slits your throat," illuminated Freddie.

"Or," suggested Hormoany, "crushes you to death and then drains the body. So Freddie's brothers aren't out to get *me*. That whole room-crushing was probably out to get you, Parry."

"Oh, I do feel so much better," said Parry.

"I wouldn't rule out Hannibal and Damian altogether," cautioned Freddie. "They might be working on commission."

"If somebody wants to drink your blood, Parry, that would mean your father must be around, or at least still alive, and if he drinks your blood he would get to be the most powerful wizard that ever existed."

"And I get to be…?" asked Parry.

"Dead," finished Freddie.

"Thanks."

"You're welcome."

"So do you reckon Jape is trying to kill me?"

"Well, it's your sire who needs to drink your blood," said Hormoany, "so he could be. But, well, what he said in the Hall made me think he could be your usurper."

"Perhaps we should keep an eye on him," said Parry, looking meaningfully over to Freddie, who was scraping bits of cheese from pizza boxes with his teeth.

"Oh right, sure, yeah," said Freddie. He looked around himself. Hormoany opened a drawer and handed Freddie the two velvet bags.

"Where might he be?" wondered Freddie.

"If we're lucky," said Hormoany, "he might be visiting your" – she caught Parry's eye – "other parent. He might be someone else at the school, too, or an outsider. If we can show Jape's plotting something with an accomplice, we can tell Bol d'Areth."

"And he'll…?"

"He'll kill 'em," said Freddie.

"I vote," said Parry, "we tell Bol d'Areth now, let him kill Jape and deal with the other one if and when he comes along."

"I don't think that's such a good idea," said Hormoany, tactfully.

"No," agreed Freddie. "You see he doesn't know who your dad is. He might simply take steps to ensure he could never drink your blood."

"Well, that's good, isn't…" started Parry.

"And kill you himself. Only way to be sure, see."

"Ah," said Parry.

Freddie raised the roving eye. "*Indfay hetum neo alledcim Jape, ae aveh ay uickqum uftish.*" The eye rose from his hand and darted out of the room. Hormoany huffed, putting her hands on her hips and her head on one side, staring at Freddie.

"Well, don't look at me," said Freddie defensively, "it wasn't *my* job to open the bloody window!"

꧁꧂

Hormoany was on her third packet of blood doughnuts by the time the roving eye had found Jape. When Freddie had discovered the command to target individuals it had been an unspoken assumption in the group that the roving eye would magically detect the whereabouts of the target, and fly there directly.

That appeared not to be the case.

Instead, the roving eye did, however, show some form of rudimentary intelligence. First, it visited Jape's office, and then Jape's apartments. Then it went to the teachers' staff room, and then the Great Hall and to the staff meeting rooms, carrying out a systematic search of the most likely places until it found him.

Hormoany squinted at the crystal ball. "Where's that, I wonder?" she asked herself as Jape strolled down an unfamiliar hallway. She grabbed a parchment from one of her desk drawers and unfurled it, using empty drinks bottles as paperweights.

"What's that?" asked Freddie.

"It's my map of the school. Let's see. The eye went down here, and oh, I see. It must be in this corridor. They've redecorated."

"What are those little moving dots?" asked Parry.

"Oh, nothing," said Hormoany, suddenly searching about herself for her wand.

"They've got a bit of writing next to them. What's that say?"

"Look, it's not important." She knocked the bottles off the scroll so that it could roll itself up, still struggling to find her wand amongst the discarded pizza boxes and food wrappers which now littered her room.

"This one," said Freddie, straightening out the scroll and peering at it, "says *'one and a half sandwiches, steak'*." He found another one. "This looks like *'one banana, one apple'*. This one says *'plate of pastries, assorted'*."

"Look, give it back!" demanded an agitated Hormoany.

"This one says *'chocolate, fruit and nut'*."

"How come the chocolate is moving?" wondered Parry.

"Not entirely sure," said Freddie.

"What are all those down there?"

One section of the map was a seething mass of labels. Freddie stared at it for a moment.

"It's hard to see with them all on top of each other like that. But I've a feeling that's the kitchen. Yes, look, that's a roast dinner, probably on its way to one of the wizards."

"You have a map," queried Parry, "that labels all the food in the school?"

"Ye-es," admitted Hormoany. "It was a gift from my sister." She finally uncovered her wand from beneath one of the take-away boxes.

"Well, that's brilliant then, isn't it?" said Parry. "All we've got to do is to convince Jape to carry round a packed lunch everywhere he goes, and we've nailed him!"

Hormoany gave Parry an unamused smile, and tapped the map with her wand. Instantly the school fare disappeared from view, leaving only the map itself.

"Hold up!" said Freddie. "I think the eye's found something."

"Where is he?" Parry asked.

"Oh, damn," complained Hormoany. "You made me miss it. Now I'll just have to try to work it out when he leaves. He can't be *that* far away," she said, glancing at the map.

and the seamy side of magic

The corridor Jape was following was dimly lit from narrow skylights. He trotted up some stone stairs.

"Must be one of the service hallways," Hormoany said.

After two flights of steps Jape stepped out into a plushly carpeted and panelled hallway. He moved down a couple of doors, knocked and waited.

"He must be in the staff quarters somewhere," said Hormoany. "I must say I don't recognize it."

The roving eye continued to approach Jape from behind. It had to be close enough to nip through the doorway if it opened – and open it did.

"Bonjour," greeted a young woman in what must have been designer underwear. "Ah, Monsieur Jape. So long since you've come to see me."

"Who the hell is she?" Parry could hardly believe his eyes.

"That's the French Mistress," Freddie informed him.

"What, she teaches French here?"

"Not teaches, exactly," replied Freddie, "but she could certainly show you a thing or two."

"What *is* he doing?" asked Hormoany, aghast.

Freddie shrugged. "Hey, they're wizards, not monks."

Jape took a long look at the French Mistress, from her auburn hair to her painted toes, where his appreciative expression froze.

"What is wrong, my darling?" asked the French Mistress. She looked down, and saw the small round shadow moving across.

Jape turned.

Freddie, Parry and Hormoany, watching the silent movie, saw Jape move suddenly, turning and stretching out his arm to the roving eye. The eye lunged forward. For a few moments it was in pink-tinged darkness, then it was approaching for a super close-up of Jape's face.

Suddenly the crystal ball itself turned into a single great eyeball. Parry, Freddie and Hormoany jumped as the eye swivelled round, looking at each of them in turn.

"Cover it up!" shouted Parry.

"Too late now, he's seen us!" said Hormoany.

But the eyeball was not focussing on them at that moment. They looked at each other, and then they followed the glassy gaze to the Grimoire of the Sorcerer Awkinsh.

"The book!" gasped Hormoany.

With a 'pop!' the book disappeared.

Under one arm, Jape held the Grimoire of Awkinsh. The roving eye was in one hand, and now in the other hand the crystal ball appeared. He gave the globe a cursory examination.

"You must excuse me, mademoiselle," said Jape, "but I fear something has come up."

"Oh please!" said the French Mistress. "I look forward to the day."

Jape dropped the roving eye into his pocket so that he could more comfortably carry both the crystal ball and the book.

Having no time for the back stairs he trotted down the main staircase and into one of the schools many lobbies. There he heard what was becoming a familiar argument, versions of which had erupted every day since the beginning of term. A girl, on this occasion a fifth-former called Liselle, was shedding angry tears at her lover's denial of their liaison. Her partner, in this case a sixth-form boy by the name of Asgard, was demanding to know what she was talking about, and insisting he had been in his dorm last night.

"Oh, do be quiet, you foolish children!" snapped Jape. "I've heard the same rows each day. Is it not clear that someone has perfected *'Merlin's Pendragon Deceit'* and, by my reckoning, must be enjoying a whale of a time? If anyone actually paid attention in my lessons you'd be forearmed against such illusions."

The emotional upset of the two lovers was suddenly turning to shocked realization and anger. "Well, who could…"

Jape continued; "Of course, whoever is doing this must be very careful not to run into whoever they are copying.

"He would need, perhaps, a crystal ball and a roving eye in order to make sure that those he copied were not going to discover him *in flagrante delicto*. Not unlike this crystal ball and roving eye I have just confiscated from a certain fifth year, by the name of – oh, yes – Hotter, Parry Hotter."

"Hotter – that was the sod who threw up on me on the train!"

"Now, if you'll excuse me," said Jape, "I have better things to do than talk to the likes of you," and he strode off.

"He's not going to get away with this," swore Asgard. "I'll kill him!"

"*Very good,*" came Jape's voice, as if from the thin air around them. "*Just don't take too long about it.*"

∽◈∾

Breakfast was very large this morning. As near as Parry could make out, it was Sunday. But the greater number of foods in front of him didn't actually increase Parry's choice a great deal, as he restricted himself to those things he could easily identify as not having once been a part of a large rat, insect or arachnid. And anyway, sleeping on Hormoany's floor had left him stiff and sore.

Hormoany's night hadn't left her much rested either. However, this had simply seemed to add a further edge to what was clearly her multi-bladed hunger. Her eyes were bloodshot, and her mood fairly foul.

"Hey, at least you were in a bed," Parry reminded her.

"Well, that didn't do me much good, did it? Every time I was about to nod off *someone* jumped on me."

Freddie was clearly enjoying his breakfast, and he sniggered.

"My roommate, Jessica, was most upset. Apparently no one touched her all night. I think that's just plain rude," she said, seeming to accuse Parry.

"What did *I* do?" asked Parry. "It was Freddie doing all the jumping."

"Exactly!" said Hormoany, resting the case for the prosecution. "And Jessica thinks she can go right off trolls."

"Oh," said Freddie. "I didn't know she was *on* trolls."

"Men!" huffed Hormoany, tucking in to something that looked as though it had five legs.

A dangerous thought crossed Freddie's mind.

"So, this blood of Parry's," he asked, "it can make a wizard really powerful, can it? You know, 'Bol d'Areth, I pull your beard and tweak your nose' sort of powerful?"

"Well, it says," said Hormoany, one greenish leg still hanging from her mouth, "that it's the power only his sire can retain. That might imply that his blood can make any wizard powerful for a time, but it definitely says only his sire will be able to retain the power."

"Right," said Freddie, staring at the long prongs of his fork. "Ri-ight."

"Ow!" screamed Parry.

"Oh, I'm sorry," said Freddie in his most innocent voice. "Let me have a look at it for you."

He pulled Parry's arm towards himself and retrieved his fork, which was sticking out of Parry's forearm.

"What are you doing? Get off me!" screamed Parry. He yanked his arm away from Freddie's mouth. There was a faint popping sound as the suction was broken.

"Just trying something," Freddie said. "A scientific experiment, if you will."

Freddie concentrated on a spoon in front of him. It hummed for a moment, lifted slowly off the table, and then launched itself, like a rocket, skyward.

From the ceiling there came a sharp crack. A few seconds later one half of a recently replaced roofing tile narrowly missed Parry and shattered on the floor. The other half of the heavy tile embedded itself in the table, a hair's breadth from Freddie himself.

"Well," said Freddie, "I'd call that experiment a success. I suppose I should have another go just to be sure."

"Put that thing down," said Parry, backing away from Freddie's vicious fork.

"It's in the name of science," reasoned Freddie.

"Science my backside!"

"Turn around then," said Freddie, fork poised. "I'm not fussy."

and the seamy side of magic 169

Something landed on Parry's head. "Aargh! Get it off me! Get it off me!" he screamed, flapping his arms at the great big bat.

"Don't do that," advised Hormoany. "If you scare him he'll only bite, and you wouldn't want him getting a taste for your blood, now would you?"

Parry froze.

"That's it," said Hormoany. "Now sit down. Good."

"Is he delivering a letter?" asked Parry.

"Well, he could be," replied Hormoany – Freddie was sniggering – "but I'm guessing by the way he's sitting on your forehead…"

"Well," explained Freddie, "I know how jealous you were of Hormoany and me getting post –"

"Parry," said Hormoany, "I think it's going to…"

"– but I didn't know what to write," continued Freddie.

The bat gave a high-pitched shriek, and deposited a not inconsiderable message on Parry's head, allowing it to drip down his face.

"Get it off me!" Parry cried.

"Dumper! Dumper!" laughed Freddie.

The bat shrieked again, and took off for a resting-place in the eaves.

"That's not funny," complained Parry.

"It depends," Freddie grinned, "where you're sitting."

Even Hormoany, who wanted to be there for Parry, couldn't help but let a smile turn up the corners of her mouth.

"I'm going to the dorm to clean off this mess," said Parry.

"Yeah. I'd better come with you," said Hormoany. "It's not safe for you to be on your own."

"It's not safe for me to be with you two, either."

Parry stomped down the corridor towards the dorms. "The look on your face," giggled Hormoany.

"It's not funny!" stressed Parry.

"If I'd known we'd have got that reaction just by letting a bat drop on his head," said Freddie, "I wouldn't have needed the bat to *drop* on his head, if you see what I mean."

"Well," said Parry, "I'm so AARGH!"

"You're so what?" asked Freddie. "Where did he go?"

"Oh Parry!" squealed Hormoany.

A couple of steps behind them, a long rectangular flagstone had disappeared from the path as Parry had stepped on it. Instinctively flinging his arms and legs out, Parry had wedged himself in the gap in a hard to maintain spread-eagled position.

"Whew," said Hormoany. "I don't like the look of those spikes. Very nasty, very nasty indeed."

"Help!" pleaded Parry. "Get me out!"

"Tricky," said Freddie, "very tricky. An action like that might upset the delicate balance you're maintaining, and then, of course, there's the element of risk involved in foiling a clearly determined murderer."

"Ooh, look at the little drain," said Hormoany. "It looks like all those spikes are drained off into that pot."

"Of course," said Freddie, "if you were willing to share some of your 'nectar of power'…"

"You blood-sucking creep!" protested Parry.

"Then again, I could just wait and collect the blood wholesale from that little pot at the bottom…"

༺❦༻

The glowing orb hung pearl-like above the pentagram in front of the kneeling figure. The swirling clouds within the orb resolved themselves into the figure of an irritated man briskly towelling his hair. "Yes?" he snapped. "What is it now?"

"The Grimoire of Awkinsh has been stolen from the Headmaster's office," said the hooded figure. "I fear the truth about the boy may be uncovered."

"Do you know who may have stolen it?"

"One called Jape was found in the vicinity, master, but the book was not in his possession."

"Why might this Jape be after the book?" asked the damp figure.

"But surely, master," said the hooded figure, "Jape is known to you. He is the boy's mother."

and the seamy side of magic

"What?" demanded He-Who-Cannot-Be-Pronounced. "Mephisto is there?"

"I assure you, master, he is a poor wizard of no consequence."

"You fool!" cried He-Who-Cannot-Be-Pronounced. "Mephisto and I vied as the most powerful wizards of our generation. It was when he sought to spy on me in the form of a woman that I was able to get him drunk and humiliate him such that he sank into the shadows.

"He has no doubt been hiding at the school for the same reason I sent you there when I discovered the existence of the child. Do not underestimate him. You'll need to deal with him at once, as he will surely stand in our way."

"It is difficult, master," said the cowled figure. "The black arts raise exotic alarms. I have devised a more subtle trap for the boy this time, but dealing with a wizard, even a third-rate one…"

"Mephisto is no third-rate wizard," warned He-Who-Cannot-Be-Pronounced. "Here, take the sword." Blade first, a sword was extended from the cloudy orb to the servant.

"Oh, thank you, master. It is my great honour to be entrusted with it."

"Well, don't break it. And I'm going to expect it back, polished. The blade is charmed and deadly, but should raise no alarm in the way casting a spell might. But I warn you, don't underestimate him. He's hidden himself for many years, but in his youth was an exceptionally powerful wizard."

"Oh, kind words indeed!" said Jape. Darkness was expelled from the room with a wave of his hand. Hanging in the air, only an arms length from the hooded figure, was the roving eye.

"Bursar, I'm surprised at you," reproached Jape.

"I don't see why," said the Bursar, pushing the hood of his robe back and revealing his face. "I am, after all, an administrator. It is in my nature to be a servant of evil."

The figure in the orb squinted. "Mephisto Orgbius! So it *is* you!"

Jape bowed. "It would seem, unpronounceable one, I can no longer hide in the shadows, but I will not let you have the boy. I would kill him first. Now if you'll excuse me, the Bursar and I have some business to conduct."

Jape dismissed He-Who-Cannot-Be-Pronounced with a gesture, bursting the luminescent globe and allowing the mist to spill out and dissipate.

"A poor choice of evil overlord, Bursar," said Jape.

"Well, there are so few choices nowadays. I might even have followed the great Mephisto, had he not been skulking in anonymity all this time, ashamed to use his own name."

Jape reached out a hand and a small object that had been sitting next to the Bursar leapt into it: a little wooden case with a door which opened to reveal a liquid-filled glass tube containing what looked like a golden ball-bearing, sized to fit the width of the tube exactly.

Jape looked at it. "An Archimedes device?" he said, with a slight smile.

The Bursar half-nodded. "Even minions must have their fun, you know."

"It's almost a shame," said Jape, "that I have to destroy you."

"Fine words from someone who's been skulking in the shadows all these years."

"Oh yes, I must thank you," said Jape. "Thanks to you, my skulking years are over."

In an instant, Jape's wand pointed at the Bursar and he cried "*Anquishvay!*" The Bursar's sword leapt in front of him, the spell distorting the very fabric of space as it deflected from the blade.

"Oh, I beg your pardon," apologised Jape. "Didn't I say '*en garde*'?"

༺❦༻

"All right! All right!" surrendered Parry.

"Eight fluid ounces," demanded Freddie, "as required."

"Yes, yes, anything."

"Anything? Twelve ounces then. What do you reckon, Hormoany?" asked Freddie. "Think you could levitate him out of there?"

and the seamy side of magic

"Not unless we change him into a piece of chalk first. How about you? Your levitation was a bit on the over-achieving side this morning."

Freddie took a coin out of his pocket. He placed in on one hand and held his wand above it. Saying the magic words he saw the coin simply shake. "No, that first little dose has worn off already."

Hormoany took off her bag, then lengthened and removed the strap. "Right!" she said, handing it to Freddie. "You get that under his chest. When you're ready I'll pull him out by the feet. You take the weight of his body."

"Yeah, yeah," said Freddie. Reaching down he found he was able to wrap the improvised rescue line around one of Parry's arms, under his chest and around the other arm. With one foot either side of the flagstones Freddie took Parry's weight as he slipped precariously close to the needle-sharp spikes below.

With Freddie supporting him, Hormoany reached down and grabbed Parry's legs, yanking them up and out of the hole, while Freddie hefted Parry's torso up.

Parry feared his face and arms were about to be impaled on the spikes as he was tipped forward. Then suddenly he was struggling for purchase on the edge of the hole, and the next moment he was scrambling clear.

The flagstone reappeared, once again disguising the trap.

"Neat trick," admired Freddie. "I imagine if you'd hit the spikes that stone would have buried you until the assassin came for your blood. You were lucky I was here to save you."

"Thanks," said Parry.

"Remember, twelve fluid ounces, on demand."

"Hey, I'm here too. I helped!" Hormoany reminded the boys.

"Thirteen fluid ounces," Freddie corrected himself.

Two battling wizards fought their way into view.

Parry, Freddie and Hormoany could barely believe their eyes.

"Who do you suppose is winning?" asked Parry.

"Well, the Bursar's advancing," offered Freddie.

"Yes," said Hormoany, "but Jape's clearly got the sword tied up in a spell from his wand. Oh, it's got free!"

The Bursar spun the sword. It seemed not even to be slowed down when it cut through concrete or metal.

"I like the way," remarked Freddie, "that Jape is using the furniture as weapons."

"Well," observed Hormoany, "half the hall furniture *is* weaponry."

Indeed, as Jape retreated, swords, spears, maces and other weapons – both those ornamenting the walls and those held by the various suits of armour along the corridor – were leaping up and throwing themselves at the Bursar. With his sword free he easily deflected them.

But each time Jape snagged the sword with a spell the Bursar seemed very vulnerable. Already, a couple of small chunks had been taken out of him.

"Honestly," cried the Bursar, "have some respect for the suit!"

"I'm sorry. I'd respect it an awful lot more if you died in it," replied Jape as he and the Bursar battled past Hormoany, Freddie and Parry's vantage point.

"Shouldn't we – you know – help one of them?" wondered Hormoany.

"I don't see why," said Parry. "Whichever way it turns out we're looking at two more free periods a week."

And that, it seemed, was not to be argued with.

"There he is!" cried Asgard, the sixth-former whose mind Jape had poisoned against Parry with false allegation. "There's the dirty little bugger!"

The lone figure was suddenly joined by something of an angry mob. The rabble carried their best Kwadwaq brooms, the ones with the nails through them. Several wands were held at the ready.

"Which one of us," asked Freddie, "do you suppose they're after?"

"Tell you what," said Parry, "I don't think I want to find out."

"Me neither."

And as the mob charged screaming 'Kill!' Parry, Freddie and Hormoany made a run for it.

A ghoul, as ghouls often are, was intrigued by the battle.

"Please," said Jape, nodding at the green figure behind the Bursar. "He's detracting from the sense of occasion."

He lowered his wand, so the Bursar had the confidence to turn to see what was happening. The ghoul loomed large behind him. Recognizing the Bursar, the man who had denied it dinner, it hissed in his face.

Automatically, the Bursar sliced through it with his sword. The ghoul, used to the entertainment of such circumstances, began to chuckle, but had hardly got the first chortle out when the lower half of its cloudy body fell to the floor. Eyes wide in alarm, the ghoul's short front arms lengthened, cartoon-like, to grab the base of its body and literally pull itself together. It fled along the corridor as if its own existence were under threat, which was probably a fair assumption.

"Thank you," said Jape. "Shall we proceed? Where were we? Ah, yes."

Again they launched into furious battle, Jape firing blast after blast, and the Bursar, swinging the sword like a man possessed, deflecting each one.

Advancing into the deadly hail of blasts and the whirlwind of the slashing sword stepped the Headmaster, spells and sword ricocheting off him. He looked up, distracted from his copy of '*The Magical Times*'. He glanced at the two staff members; Jape, his wand behind his back, the Bursar with the sword behind his.

"Morning," the Headmaster grunted.

"Good morning, sir," nodded the two men.

And with that the Headmaster, oblivious to the circumstances, strolled on.

"Now, where were we again?" asked Jape.

The Bursar screamed as he charged, bringing the sword down towards Jape's head.

"Ah, yes," said Jape, wand raised in defence.

"Now, are you sure?" asked Gordon. The little squealer plant repeatedly jabbed its spiky leaves towards the door. "Well, if you're quite certain."

Plant pot in one hand, Gordon pushed the door. The room had a pentagram inscribed across the floor. Discarded to one side lay the Archimedes device.

"Interesting," remarked Gordon, taking in the layout. "I wonder if I should try, '*astlim umbernas edialras*'?"

୨∞୧

By the time Jape and the Bursar had fought their way to the Great Lobby, even the suits of armour had given up their sentry-like positions and were backing off into other rooms, corridors and the adjoining hall; a couple were even sneaking away down the service stairs and one used the main door, leaving it slightly ajar.

Both men now carried bloody injuries, some of Jape's projectiles having clearly struck home, and equally the Bursar having slashed Jape's leg and across his chest.

"You're growing tired, old man," sneered the Bursar. "You can't keep the spell rate or the strength up, can you? You've let your abilities rust."

With a lightning thrust the Bursar caught Jape's wand with his sword. The wand whipped out of Jape's hand and clattered across the floor. Jape lunged, as if to try and recover it, but the sword was at his throat.

"It was a fine battle, my dear friend," said the Bursar, "but all good things…"

"You fool," said Jape. "Strike me down now, I'll become more powerful than you could ever imagine."

"Mm," said the Bursar, considering this. "Let's see. Would I really like to have you as some disembodied voice whispering your little thoughts in some teenager's ear, or have you fully embodied and waiting to turn me into fish food when I'm not looking?"

He swung the sword viciously and powerfully around his head, and then brought it cutting down through Jape's torso. It sliced through Jape's robe like a hot knife through butter – and met no resistance as it passed from shoulder to waist. The robe collapsed, empty, to the floor.

The Bursar tested the robe with his foot, revealing the end of Jape's wand protruding from one of the robe's sleeves.

The Bursar glanced to where he believed the wand had fallen when he had knocked it out of Jape's hand. It wasn't there. He looked back at the wand in the robe. "Hm," he said, and bent down and picked up the wand.

It was an impressive wand, intricately carved ebony wood revealing the ivory of unicorn horn in its centre. "A most pleasant souvenir," said the Bursar, giving the wand a practice wave.

Suddenly, serpent-like, the wand wrapped itself around the Bursar's hand. The man cried out in pained surprise as his hand was crushed. Then the wand thrust black and white roots deep into his flesh.

"No!" he cried. He was on his knees. The sword was his only hope. He tried to raise it in his left hand. If he could only hack his right arm off fast enough...

But even as the Bursar raised his sword, black and white tendrils exploded from his left hand. He screamed as he fell backward, the tendrils bursting out of his arms, legs, stomach, throat, face. By now his right arm was in a shimmering state of flux; as quickly as his agonized screams faded his whole body joined the nightmarish in-between existence.

From the indistinct mass that was the Bursar's body a lump detached itself and fell to the floor. It resolved as an emaciated figure of skin and bone alone, naked and dead on the floor, then the animated figure solidified itself.

Jape wore the Bursar's damaged clothes, but he filled them more powerfully than either of the men could have done before. He looked at his strong hands, the powerful frame he now inhabited. He walked to the mirror and gazed into it.

"I remember you," said the reflection.

"Indeed," said the figure. "Jape is no more. I, Mephisto, am back!"

Gordon followed the trail of destruction along one corridor and then the next, tutting at the damage to floors and walls where medieval weapons jutted out and lumps of stone had been hacked away. He stepped around those parts of the floor where stone tiles had been changed by transfiguring blasts to molten metal, now cooling, or pools of acid, still very dangerous.

He tentatively made his way into the Great Lobby. He saw suits of armour peering around doorways, themselves checking the coast was clear, before creeping back to their rightful positions.

He checked on the cold and emaciated form lying on the ground. Picking up the damaged and discarded robe that had belonged to Jape, he lay it over the body to give it some dignity.

As he covered the body's head he noticed something staring at him.

Lying by the wall, where it had fallen when its master had been cut down, was the roving eye. Gordon picked it up. Bringing his fist to his forehead he concentrated for a moment. "Now, what have you been up to, Jape," Gordon wondered.

"*Ightlium ingersfay*," he muttered under his breath. A small box appeared in his hand. He flicked the lid open, and admired the jewelled contents. He dropped them into one pocket. He concentrated again, and a very fine set of celestial spheres appeared. He put them on the floor, and concentrated once more. The Grimoire of the Sorcerer Awkinsh appeared in his hand.

"This," Gordon thought aloud, "should make interesting reading."

Being one of the more athletic sportsmen at Warthogs, sixth-former Avedum was the first to catch up with our fleeing band. Hormoany had a fair lead, and although wilting a little, Parry was second. But Freddie who, let's say, wasn't built for long-distance running, was lagging behind, so it was he whom the sixth-former grabbed.

"I've got one of them," Avedum shouted, wrestling with Freddie. As one, they glanced back. The pack was certainly pursuing them, but it must be said, at more of a quick jog than an outright run. In fact, considering the amount of ground they had to cover, they were still perhaps a minute or two away.

It was then that Avedum realized how, in his enthusiasm for the chase, he had made a critical error of judgment. Freddie was, after all, a Weasel, and the Weasel family – although, it had to be admitted, not built for sprinting – *were* built for pulling arms and legs off people. Freddie easily pulled the nail-studded Kwadwaq broom from Avedum's hand and smiled an evil Freddie Weasel smile.

§

Gordon placed the tea service by his desk. He poured a cup of tea through the tea strainer, and popped in a slice of lemon. The Grimoire of Awkinsh sat on his desk, alongside his Concise Dictionary of Ancient Languages and a pad of paper with an enchanted quill poised to take notes.

The grandfather clock counted out the time; tick tock, tick tock.

"This," said Gordon, "will take a little time."

Tick tock, tick. Tock.

Tick.

Gordon busied himself. He switched some lights on, then he went out to the kitchen and brought back a small platter of fondant fancies. The skies outside seemed to dim.

Tock.

"That's better," said Gordon.

Two minutes passed, according to the great clock. But of course we know that clocks can be a very poor measure of subjective time.

A pile of notes sat by Gordon's right hand, almost as thick as the Grimoire itself. "Interesting," said Gordon, "very interesting."

He stood up and turned out one of the lights. Something outside caught his eye. Moving over to the window he squinted through the twilight.

There, seemingly frozen like statues, were Hormoany and Parry, and a little behind them was the apparently stationary Freddie carrying a bloodied Kwadwaq broom. And if you looked carefully you could see the angry mob, pursuing imperceptibly slowly, a comfortable distance behind.

Tick, said the clock behind him.

"Dear, dear, dear," said Gordon to the slow motion figures. He went into his kitchen and to the back door. Inside his small old-fashioned conservatory he changed into his gardening shoes, pulled on a pair of gloves, and ran his finger down the edge of a number of packets of seeds. "Yes, these will do nicely," he thought.

Tock.

※

Golf is not a game that wizards play very often. Wizards enjoy games of skill and wit. However, it took very little skill or wit to charm a golf ball into heading straight for a hole, and then every tee shot was a hole in one, and then all eighteen holes played with a single stroke. The game somewhat lost its appeal.

There had been rare attempts where wizards were on their honour to play a fair game of golf like the mortals, but these usually broke down with vicious, and largely justified, accusations of cheating.

But in the corner of Bol d'Areth's office sat a brand new set of golf clubs. He tried an iron. Taking it out of the bag he putted an imaginary ball. He seemed satisfied.

He shouldered the club, and then swung it thoughtfully at head height until it was behind his other shoulder. Then he looked carefully at the club, went back to the bag and took out a driver instead. He slipped the club out of its protective cover and regarded the large wooden head and deep face. He tried one or two gentle head-height swings.

"Much better," the Headmaster said to himself.

The pursuing pack was maintaining a comfortable distance between itself and Freddie, Parry and Hormoany. They all agreed in principle that they must chase these three villains down, but in practice they'd all seen what had happened to Avedum. So frankly, none of them wanted to be the first to catch up with Freddie, which meant they'd covered almost the whole distance between the school building proper and the rear of Gordon's own private gardens at a comfortable trot.

Gordon came around the corner of his house, pushing his old wooden wheelbarrow full of gardening tools and compost, wearing his floppy sunhat, his gardening gloves and favourite gardening shoes.

"Careful," he warned Hormoany, Parry and Freddie. "Those are man-eating pansies, and I should know."

Hormoany trotted along the narrow gap between the flowers, but was through before many of them woke up to her presence.

They were more alert for Parry and snapped at him like miniature pastel Rottweilers. Despite the warning, Parry was taken by surprise. He jumped back from a row of tiny gnashing teeth, simply in shock as, in fact, they couldn't reach him. However, jumping back landed him in the opposite bed, where his ankles were promptly mauled. Dancing like a hyper-animated Pinocchio, Parry just made it to the safety of Gordon's side of the flowerbed.

Freddie at least, in his thick, heavy hide mountain-boots, had some degree of protection, but he still had to stomp off one or two flowers which had sunk their teeth into the leather and been uprooted as he ran through them.

"Piranhas of the flora kingdom," said Gordon proudly. "I was highly commended at last year's show."

"Oh, that makes me feel a lot better," said Parry, "knowing they're award-winning."

"Well," said Gordon, looking past him, "I think if I'd had those to enter I would have got *first* prize."

Parry looked over his shoulder. Several of the plants were already two or three times the size they had been. One was already at waist height, and growing fast.

The mob, however, were cycling through various states of group psychology: the main priority was, of course, to lynch Parry and his friends, although with a wizard right there it seemed unlikely that they would reach that outcome.

But on the plus side, it seemed equally unlikely that, as a group, they would suffer a pounding at the hands of Freddie Weasel. And those who survived to tell the tale would undoubtedly fall foul of Freddie's brothers who, after all, had a reputation to maintain: a hard-earned and viciously won reputation, at that.

Those without a very personal grievance thought honour could be satisfied at this point with a lot of shouting and waving of fists. They had, after all, chased them halfway round the school, and over the playing fields. Surely, punishment enough.

Those with a personal grievance reckoned Parry might be easier to sort out when he was on his own.

"Giant man-eating pansies," called Gordon to the lynch mob, as he busied himself taking off his gardening gloves and finding some rubber ones.

"Hotter raped Abigail, Catherine and Liselle, and heaven knows who else!" cried an accuser from the crowd.

"Really?" said Gordon. "Do mind the giant man-eating pansies. And just how did he manage these dreadful deeds?"

"He used *'Merlin's Pendragon Deceit'* spell," a member of the mob replied. "We're going to lynch him!"

"You *have* been a busy boy, are you going for Sade House captain?" an amused Gordon teased Parry.

"It's time for him to pay," threatened Asgard, pointing an accusing finger at Parry. A pansy, standing head and shoulders above him, took that as an invitation. With one chomp Asgard no longer had a right arm.

"Oh *really*, I did warn you," reproached Gordon.

Two of Asgard's braver fellows waded into the pansies with their Kwadwaq brooms to beat a path to retrieve him. He stood in shock, staring at the stump where his arm had been. The giant pansy was shaking the arm like a dog with a rag doll.

"Small or giant, they're just the same," tutted Gordon. "Eyes bigger than their digestive cavities."

Asgard was dragged away from the pansies. His companions had lost a broom when one of the giant plants had grabbed it and wrestled it out of their hands, but apart from that and some ankle wounds they were largely undamaged.

"Now really," said Gordon seriously, "this child had never heard of magic a week ago. I think it's just a teensy-weensy bit far-fetched to imagine he has mastered Merlin's most accomplished feat of wizardry in a little under seven days, don't you? Magically speaking, this boy can't even tie his own shoelaces yet. What on earth gave you that silly idea?"

"Well," said an embarrassed voice. "Jape said…"

Gordon's eyebrows shot up. "This would be the same Jape who holds Parry's birth against him, and who tried to kill him the other evening at dinner? Hmm?"

There was an embarrassed shuffling of feet, accompanied by wincing from those whose feet were heavily lacerated.

"Now, I do suggest you get yourselves off to the infirmary. Mr Tollopoff will bandage your feet, and I'm sure he'll fix Asgard up with an arm as good as new, wooden, yes, but fully functional. It's amazing what that man can do with enchanted wood. I'd take my hat off to him, but the sun is no good for my complexion."

"But if it wasn't him…?" wondered one of the crowd.

"I'll tell you what," reassured Gordon, "I'll keep an eye out for you. Now do run along."

Gordon waited a few moments to be sure the mob were really moping back to the school before he addressed Hormoany, Parry and Freddie. "Now, I think you'd probably better come inside. I'll be along in a minute," he said, glancing at the giant pansy that was ripping up its roots and trying out some '*The Day of the Triffids*' style shuffling, "once I've dealt with our friends here. I expect that'll be due to your 'nectar of power', Parry."

The three of them looked at him, suddenly realizing what he had said.

Hormoany was the first to speak. "You know about the prophecy?"

"Let's just say, I made some time to do a little reading. Now, inside the house please, before you're all plant food. And please stop bleeding on the grass, Parry. You know it's simply a nightmare to cut. And what is that stuff in your hair? Now, where did I leave my flame thrower?"

◆◆◆

Reverently, Artorius Smudge and the wizard Jarvaris lay the Bursar's body out on a stone slab in the morgue, pulling a white sheet over him.

"No, I'll tell the Headmaster myself. He'll know if there's any family to contact." Artorius shook his head. "Dear oh dear."

The two wizards left one torch burning in the cold room, and trotted back up the worn stone steps, closing the mortuary door behind them.

From the shadows came a tall figure. He slipped the dark hood away from his face, and stepped into the pool of light that bathed the Bursar's body.

"Well, well, well," said He-Who-Cannot-Be-Pronounced. "It certainly makes a change for me to call on you when you're indisposed."

◆◆◆

The Headmaster watched the storm cloud roll in from the northeast, to the accompaniment of lightning flashes and rolls of thunder.

That in itself wasn't too unusual.

The fact that this particular storm cloud had come alone – in an otherwise clear sky – that *was* fairly unusual. And the way it hovered over the school's eastern wing – 'That,' thought Bol d'Areth, 'is never a good sign.'

and the seamy side of magic

He just wished he could remember whether the conversation he'd had with Gordon about it was something he'd already done, or was going to do.

✦

"Look at this," said Hormoany. "This looks like the Amulet of Eynmanfus." She tried to lift the ornate metal buckle but found it impossible to move from the mantelpiece. "Wow! It really is as heavy as they say, and this," she looked at a wand hovering in the centre of a glass case, "this says it's the Wand of Midas. That's amazing!"

Gordon strode back into the room, brushing flecks of ash from his jacket with his hands. "Oh dear," he said, "you haven't made yourselves at home at all."

Parry was perched on the edge of a chair examining his wounded feet. Freddie stood awkwardly in the middle of the room, on the basis that he wouldn't sit on a chintz sofa as a matter of principle.

Hormoany had been admiring Gordon's trophies. "Oh, you know," he said, "when you've been around a while you tend to collect a few beautiful things." He picked up the Amulet of Eynmanfus and dusted it before returning it to the mantelpiece. The three of them had spotted the Grimoire of Awkinsh.

"I'm sure the *'Antiques Road Show'* is very interesting and all," said Parry, "but I think there's a little something we're forgetting here? Mad wizards trying to kill me?"

"Well," said Gordon, passing him a first aid kit, "at least Jape's not trying to do it himself. He probably knows that Bol d'Areth and I have strict rules regarding the murdering of pupils. Only with proper authorisation."

"Authorisation, yes, *that's* the issue here?"

"He probably just doesn't want you to fall into the hands of your father, Parry."

There was a bang at the door. Gordon moved the curtain aside a little. "Of course, I could be wrong about that. Stay here."

Gordon went to the front door and opened it. He had to look twice. "Jape?" he asked.

"I have done with that name now," said Jape. "I am Mephisto."

"If you've come for the boy, you can't have him."

"If I'd come for the boy," said Jape, "you would by now be no better off than the Bursar."

"Dear, dear," said Gordon, "I was going to ask you about that…"

"The Bursar served He-Who-Cannot-Be-Pronounced. It was necessary. Give the boy this." Jape handed Gordon a neck-chain. On the chain was a medallion set with a glowing red stone.

"Now," said Gordon, "if I've understood correctly, the last amulet you gave this boy was designed to blow his head off when he popped it in his mouth."

"I was weak then," snarled Jape. "Had I my strength, I would have destroyed the child rather than live in shame and ignominy for these many years. But now my darkness is passed. The child is not my enemy, but the evil wizard who inflicted him on me is. The amulet is charmed, and will protect the boy.

"He-Who-Cannot-Be-Pronounced will be coming. He needs the child's blood, and I don't wish him to have it. The amulet will serve two purposes. It will protect the boy, and it will warn me. Don't kid yourself, gardener. I am the boy's only chance."

"*He* is the sire?" asked Gordon.

"Indeed," answered Jape bitterly, "and I shall be avenged." He turned on his heels and left.

Gordon closed the door, examining the amulet. He waved his hand across it. For a moment Parry thought he saw a glimpse of silver.

"Well, well, well!" said Gordon. "It does exactly what it says on the tin." He offered the amulet to Parry.

"Get off!" said Parry. "I'm not wearing that!"

"Put it this way," Gordon told him, "if He-Who-Cannot-Be-Pronounced does find you, this will improve your chances considerably."

"Why, what are my chances now?"

"Mm, let me see. I'd say, none."

Hormoany snatched the amulet from Gordon's hand and threw it quickly around Parry who, still bandaging his feet, was too slow to react.

"There, it's on, and we've got to go now," she said urgently.

"Why?" asked Freddie.

"What's wrong?" Parry asked.

"Are you both mad?" demanded Hormoany. "It's lunchtime!"

CHAPTER 10

The mortuary door splintered and burst open. Bare feet padded down the cold hard floor of the corridor. The four wizards were chatting, wondering who could have done such a thing, and saying he was a decent chap, really. An excellent Bursar, and where would they find a replacement?

Cold eyes assessed each wizard's garb. Too small, too large, last year's style.

The fourth was a match.

"Give me your clothes, now!" came the command.

The wizards looked at him in shock.

"Bursar?" asked one.

"I need your clothes. Remove them. Give them to me."

"Great to see you up and about, old man. We're going to have to get you to the infirmary. We thought you were a goner."

"Your clothes," snapped the Bursar, "now!" He grabbed the wizard with one hand and hurled him across the hall, slamming him into the stone wall.

"I say, steady on!"

"Your clothes," demanded the Bursar, grabbing him again, and slamming him into the opposite wall. The wizard fell motionless to the ground.

His three compatriots glanced at one other and raised their wands in unison.

"*Anquishvay!*" they cried simultaneously. But the spell, designed for mortal and immortal foe, was a damp squib against undead flesh. The wizards never got an opportunity for a second shot.

"That's just great, isn't it? I'm related to the lunatic Jape and to someone whose name I can't even pronounce – no one can even pronounce. I mean, what's the story with that?"

"It's Welsh, I think," volunteered Hormoany.

Parry turned on Hormoany, catching his drink with an elbow and knocking it to the floor. "Oh great! Now I'm going to have to find my roots by taking an interest in rugby and choral singing." Blaming Hormoany, he ducked under the table to retrieve his mug.

At that moment the Bursar entered. He cast his cold dead eyes across the main tables. His quarry was not visible. He would bide his time. The Bursar began moving between the tables, tidying place settings as he went.

Parry came back up.

Freddie said, "Didn't Jape – "

"He likes to be called Mephisto now," interrupted Hormoany.

"Yes," said Freddie. "Didn't Jape say the Bursar was working with the guy with the funny name?"

"That's right," said Hormoany. "He-Who-Cannot-Be-Pronounced."

"And didn't he say he was dead?"

"Yeah."

"Then why," asked Freddie, "is he over there?"

"Wow!" enthused Hormoany, "I'll bet he's an *avatar*! You know, an undead agent of another? Oh, what's the muddled term…?"

"Zombie?" suggested Parry despondently.

"Yes, that's it!" agreed Hormoany excitedly, "a zombie! So this would be the Bursar*atar*!" She paused a few moments, deflating a little. "It's not likely to be good news, is it?"

The lifeless eyes of the Bursaratar met Parry's. Immediately he started coming straight at the young apprentice. The fact that there was a table in the way didn't seem to mean very much to him. He threw the seated diners in the air as he reached them and slammed his fist through the table, pounding on it, aiming to break it up to allow him a straight line at Parry.

Parry and Freddie took a more practical decision and leapt over their table to follow Hormoany full-pelt to the door.

The three reached the sports pavilion. "Do you think he's still after us?" wondered Parry anxiously.

"Well, let's see," said Freddie. "He's a zombie, and he hasn't got us yet. Yeah, I reckon he's still after us."

Hormoany stuck her head out from behind the bin where they were hiding. "And I can see him," she added.

Parry stuck his head round the next corner. "Right," he said, "this is very, very important. If someone left a flying broom around – "

"It's no good," said Freddie, "you need the password. Everyone sets their own, and the school changes it every day to stop them getting nicked after each lesson."

"Yes, be that as it may," said Parry. "But what if someone had left a broom hovering when they had finished their flying lesson. What command do you need to make it go?"

Hormoany replied, "*Alkway noium.*"

"And what would you say to make it go really fast?" asked Parry.

Hormoany shrugged. "*Iddygium pu ae allopgus.*"

"Right," said Parry decisively. He stood up and, reaching around the corner, pulled a floating broom into view. He threw one leg over it, taking a good grip of the handle and pointing it out towards the playing fields, directly away from the oncoming Bursaratar.

"It's been nice knowing you. Don't forget to write. *Alkway noium, Iddygium pu ae allopgus!*" he commanded.

"But wait!" cried Hormoany. But Parry was already gone. The broom accelerated immediately, although, from Parry's point of view, backwards.

"Why is it," asked Hormoany, "that the muddled people think brooms fly handle forward?"

"Beats me," said Freddie, "but it's not half going to hit the Bursar hard."

It did.

Dead brains react a little more slowly than live ones, and the Bursaratar barely had time to register the brush coming towards him and the teenager sitting backward on the broom, before he was struck.

and the seamy side of magic

The broom lifted him off the ground, and the two of them went slamming into a wall. Fortunately for Parry, the Bursaratar cushioned his impact. Parry lay stunned for a few moments. Freddie and Hormoany jogged up.

"You all right?" asked Freddie, pulling Parry to his feet.

"Where am I?"

"Look at the Bursaratar," said Hormoany.

The Bursar's flesh was torn, one eye barely hanging in its socket, the skin of one arm ripped away.

"Nasty, said Freddie. "Well, at least – "

The Bursar's body jolted.

"Oh, dear," said Hormoany, "I think we'd better…"

The Bursaratar sat up.

"– *RUN*!" screamed the three teenagers together.

And they did.

The Bursaratar pulled himself to his feet. Lurching forward, he found was dragging his left foot. Looking down and lifting his robe, he could see the bone jutting awkwardly through his skin. He dragged himself forward regardless, until he caught sight of his reflection in a window. Tutting, he dusted down his robe and straightened it out a little.

He looked carefully at the reflection of his face.

Shattering a window with his hand, he took a sharp shard of glass and cut out the damaged eye. An unearthly glow emanated from the empty socket. Then he sliced away the shredded skin from his right hand, leaving only bone and sinew.

The Bursaratar peered through the broken window. He was looking into one of the school's many workshops. Enchanted swords and diabolical devices didn't (usually) just forge themselves, after all. Seeing protective clothing, he reached through and pulled out a pair of welding goggles and a glove. He donned the glove on his damaged hand, and the smoked glass of the goggles disguised the glow from his empty eye. Satisfied, he limped off in pursuit of his quarry.

༄༅

At the speed Hormoany, Parry and Freddie tore between the outbuildings very little could stop them.

Very big, however, *could* stop them.

"Well, well, well!" said Damian. "It seems you're very lucky to run into us at this moment in time."

"An auspicious event," said Hannibal.

"Without a doubt," agreed Damian, "very lucky indeed."

"For us?" asked Hormoany suspiciously, picking herself off the floor, "or for the Bursaratar back there?"

"Tut, tut, tut," reproached Damian.

"Really," said Hannibal, "some people always see the worst in others."

"We," said Damian, "are here to help. We understand that our good friend Parry's blood here can be quite a valuable commodity."

"Valuable, indeed," said his brother.

"However, we understand a certain sire is trying to corner the market in Parry blood."

"Dear, dear, dear," said Hannibal. "Very bad for business, as indeed our understanding is that if a certain individual gets all of Parry's blood…"

"Vis-à-vis, our Bursaratar friend there."

"…then this certain individual will become all-powerful."

Damian tutted. "Very bad for business, is that."

"Very bad indeed," said Hannibal.

"If we're talking ruthless evil dictator here," said Damian, "rather than Bol d'Areth's benign governance, we may find business conditions deteriorate. Malevolent omnipotent dictators are not famous for their kind disposition towards the smaller…"

"…up and coming…"

"entrepreneur. Or as we like to say, it's the wrong 'm.o.'."

"Nice as it is to stand around chatting with you guys," said Parry, "but there *is* a zombie on our tail and he'll be here any minute."

"I'd say," said Hannibal, checking in the crystal ball drawn from his pocket, "about three minutes. You see that walk, brother," he said.

Damian peered into the glass. "He's got that slow, purposeful walk..."

"Purposeful walk," echoed Hannibal.

"...limp," Damian corrected himself, "the kind where no matter how fast you run he'll always be just behind you."

"Exactly," said Parry, "so if you don't mind..."

"He'll keep coming," said Damian, "until he gets you."

"That's what he does," agreed Hannibal.

"That's *all* he does," warned Damian.

"So will you please get out of my way?" implored Parry.

"But we," said Damian, "can protect you."

"For a small consideration," said Hannibal, "maybe, oh, eight ounces of blood..."

"Payable bi-monthly," clarified Damian.

"...indefinitely, we will be able to deal with this imminent threat to your life. Under a minute and a half, I'd say," said Hannibal, referring back to the crystal ball. "He really does seem a very determined avatar."

"Okay, okay!" agreed a pressurized Parry.

"A very wise decision," said Hannibal.

"All transactions final." Damian yanked open a heavy metal door set in the wall. "You'll be safe in here while we attend to business."

The three of them were bundled through the door. The door slammed behind them. It took a moment for their eyes to adjust to the dim light. Then they could see the machinery, a huge wall of machinery practically the height of the workshop itself.

"What is this place?" asked Hormoany.

"Ah, this," supposed Freddie, "will be the print works, for '*The Sol*', I do imagine."

"I see. And this would be?" she indicated half a dozen crystal balls and half dozen horn-like shells.

A couple of the crystal balls had roving eyes hanging over them, others showed images from various places around the school. One crystal ball stand was empty, presumably waiting for the one Hannibal was carrying. Next to them were rows of horn-like shells. A couple of them had smaller snail-like shells hanging in the air above them, while others were relaying back conversations of those that could be seen in the crystal balls for a busy set of enchanted quills to transcribe.

"Newsgathering," Freddie surmised.

"Right," said Hormoany, snatching one of the roving eyes out of the air and handing it to Freddie, "let's keep an eye on what your brothers are doing."

୨୦୧

Damian and Hannibal had set themselves up a hundred paces or so toward the main building where they considered the pathway suitably narrow.

"This'll do. Two charges should be adequate," said Damian, setting down a couple of solid, square brown paper blocks. He pulled out some faded parchment. Hannibal glanced at his crystal ball, and he set it down beside him, pulling out a similar envelope from his pocket.

"Two ounces of dehydrated aqua," said Hannibal, pouring the contents of the packet into the top of the charge.

"And one ounce of activated phosphorus," said Damian, pouring his into the mixture. "That should give us about fifty-five seconds."

"That's odd," said Hannibal. "I don't remember the timing mixture smoking quite like that."

"Are you sure," queried Damian, "that was two ounces?"

"Yeah, of course I'm sure, I used the new scales acquired from Master Hotter only last week."

"They wouldn't by any chance be calibrated to the avoirdupois system, would they?"

"Oh, I see the problem. If you've used the old apothecaries' weights, that would mean…"

Kahboom!!!

The Bursaratar trudged through the burning debris. He paused at the edge of the shallow crater, inspecting the body of Damian on one side, and Hannibal on the other. A charred brown cube lay smouldering in his path. He tried to smother the burning object by kicking a little earth over it.

Kahboom!!!

The flaming figure struggled a few steps and fell on to all fours, then on to its side, and finally came to rest on its back.

It was some minutes before Hormoany, Parry and Freddie tentatively approached the two craters and three bodies.

"I'm sorry about your brothers," commiserated Parry. "Do you suppose he's dead?"

"What, the Bursar?" clarified Freddie. "Yeah, he's dead. The question is, is he un-undead?"

"I think," said Hormoany, "my guess would be Option C," pointing at the skeletal figure rising from the ashes, "incredibly pissed-off."

As one, they screamed "Run!" The trio bolted into the printing room and slammed the heavy metal door.

"Bolt it!" screamed Parry.

"I *have* bolted it," replied Freddie.

"Bolt it some more!"

There came a tap at the door.

Tap, tap, tap.

The three of them looked at one another.

Tap, tap, tap.

Hormoany looked at the door. She spotted the small eye-plate.

Tap, tap, tap.

She took the catch off the eye-plate, and opened the tiny door.

Through the grille a skull was staring, a malevolent red light in the empty socket.

"I wish to see Parry Hotter," said a voice.

"Since when," asked Freddie, "was the Bursar German?"

"You can't see him," called Parry. "And even if you could, he isn't here."

"I see," said the cold voice from the other side of the door. "I'll be back," said the voice, "forthwith."

"I don't like the sound of that," said Parry.

"Forthwith?" said Hormoany helpfully. "That only means 'soon'."

"I meant the other part."

"Why," wondered Freddie, "do you suppose we've locked ourselves into a building with no back door?"

Parry and Hormoany turned around. The small skylights were impossibly high, and the whole rear wall of the small room was one mass of printing machinery.

"Surely some spell…" supposed Parry.

"Tricky," said Freddie. "Most spells don't work on the undead."

"So you're saying we've only got a couple of minutes to live?"

Parry and Freddie looked at one another. Then they looked at Hormoany, and back at one another. Freddie pulled a coin out of his pocket, and tossed it. "I got heads," he said.

"Right," said Parry. Both boys lunged for Hormoany, Freddie grabbing her hair and pulling her down, Parry grabbing at her waist and trying to get behind her.

The fury of her response surprised both boys. In a moment Freddie was nursing a deep bite wound and Parry was trying to stand with what felt like a dislocated kneecap.

"What was that for?" demanded Freddie.

"A lady," said Hormoany sternly, "likes to be asked."

About four paces to one side of the reinforced metal door the wall burst in. A flying broom, brushwood snapping, came crashing through, carrying the Bursaratar.

Wads of paper, packets and supplies went flying.

Freddie was first with his wand. "*Anquishvay! Anquishvay! Anquishvay!*" he fired off, but the spells were like pinpricks to the skeletal Bursaratar.

"Quick, Parry!" Freddie cried. "Get a knife! I need more power! Open one of your arteries!"

Hormoany, meanwhile, had snatched up a couple of the explosive charges that had been scattered on the floor as the Bursaratar burst in. Now she was desperately scouring the room for some form of cover – a trapdoor, or – she spotted the grille over the main conveyor of the printing press.

She tugged on the grille, but it wouldn't budge. Looking around the edges she found the bolt. Releasing it she opened the grille. There was just room for them to crawl inside.

"Quickly!" she screamed. "In here!"

Freddie maintained the rate of fire from his wand – while Parry continued pelting the Bursaratar with bricks – as they backed into the narrow gap.

"Quickly! Quickly!" Hormoany urged. "Parry, give me your wand!"

Freddie bundled himself inside, and started scrambling along on his stomach. Parry followed, handing his wand to Hormoany as he threw his last brick.

The Bursaratar, struggling on the uneven floor with his gammy leg, kept dragging himself towards them.

Hormoany sat herself inside the machine and pushed Parry's wand into the charge in place of a detonator.

She grabbed Parry's foot as he tried to squirm away and, ripping the bandage off, sucked on his ankle. She turned back just as the Bursaratar was reaching for her hiding-place.

"*Anquishvay!*" she screamed. The Bursaratar's arm was thrown backwards as the sheer force of the wand blast spun him around. She thrust the explosive charge, held like a lolly on Parry's wand, into his rib cage, and dropped down the steel shutter.

"*Etonated!*"

The explosion was deafening.

"What happened?" cried Freddie.

"Pardon?" said Parry.

"What?" said Hormoany.

"What happened?" called Freddie again.

"Speak up," requested Hormoany.

"What happened?" he called.

"Never mind," said Hormoany. "I can't hear you. I think," she said, peering through the gaps in the shutter, "I got him."

She could see a skeletal leg on the debris at one side of the room, and a hip and a portion of leg a few yards away.

"Yeah, I think I got him," she said again.

"What?" asked Parry.

She tentatively edged the shutter up.

A bony hand grabbed on to the metal framework, then another bony hand. The Bursar's skull drew into view, a murderous glow in its eyes and an evil fixed smile across its broken teeth.

Hormoany kicked out as hard as she could, knocking the hellishly persistent torso away. She started scrabbling as fast as she could through the machinery. Moments later, the remains of the Bursaratar had dragged themselves back up, thrown open the shutter once more and was pulling itself along on its hands and elbows after them.

Parry scrambled out of the other side of the machine. "Now what?" he gasped.

"Run!" suggested Freddie.

"No!" cried Hormoany. "This ends here."

The Bursaratar pulled himself forward, and forward again.

"I'll make you regret the day you ever messed with Judicita Harmonica!" she cried.

She dropped the safety grille at her end of the machine, just as the bony fingers thrust out towards her.

She stabbed the green '*Start*' button at the side of the machine. There was an agonizing wait as the machinery hissed and rumbled into life. "Sayonara, baby!"

The Bursar's skull had its glowing eye sockets fixed on Hormoany, but then the mechanical noises began to distract the zombie. The Bursaratar looked around, as if for the first time assessing his position. For a moment, as much as a skeleton could, he seemed agitated, and desperately tried to push himself backwards. But then the great printing press came crashing down, once, *crack!* twice, *crack!* three times, *shatter!*

It was some time before Hormoany chose to hit the red '*Stop*' button. The three of them peered into the gloom of the machine at the shattered bone.

"What do you suppose we should do with him now?" asked Parry.

"I expect we leave that to the wizards. Imagine there'd be a decent funeral," thought Freddie.

"He is dead, I suppose," said Parry.

"Mind you, he was dead before."

Hormoany found what she was looking for amongst the printing supplies. She hefted up a huge container marked '*Plate Acid*'.

"Good idea," nodded Parry.

୨୦୧

"An unfortunate turn of events," said the first disembodied voice.

"Yes, quite an unfortunate turn of events, brother," agreed the second voice. "But we do have a contract."

"Indeed," agreed the first voice. "And where there is commerce, there is hope."

୨୦୧

"Careful!" warned Hormoany. "It's eating through the tin. Don't let it splash you."

The boys held the drum over the drain for as long as they could, before the metal of the drum became so paper-thin it began to collapse under its own weight. The bottom lip of the drum had dissolved away, and the drum itself slumped like a crushed tin can on the floor.

Hormoany watched as the stout metal grille covering the drain hissed and dissolved, the metal dropping into the drain itself.

"Wow! That *is* strong stuff," said Parry.

"Probably got an efficiency spell on it," speculated Hormoany. The boys pulled off their thick hide gloves and aprons, which they had found conveniently stored by the plate acid, and left them on a pile by the drain.

The three of them turned for the walk back to the main building.

"Sorry about your brothers," consoled Hormoany.

"Yeah," agreed Parry. "They were all right."

"No," said Freddie, "they weren't, but they *were* my brothers. When I start in the protection and racketeering business, it will be in memory of them."

"Did anyone else hear that sloshing sound?" asked Parry.

"You mean that damp, oozing sound?" clarified Hormoany.

"Yeah, and that slapping sound, like wet cloth hitting a stone floor. Is that usual?"

"I don't think so."

"And I was really hoping," complained Parry, "that Jape was going to be the only thing I had to worry about now. Do you think we'd better turn round?"

"Well, one of us should. I vote it's you, Hormoany. Ladies first."

"And they say chivalry is dead. That's not the half of it. How about if we all turn round on the count of three? One, two, three! Come on boys, we're only delaying the inevitable."

Slowly they turned their heads around to the source of the slurping noise.

Welling up from the drain was a liquid man, given a whitish tint from the dissolved bone and a silvery hue from the dissolved metal.

The watery nightmare stared at its arm as its hand flowed into shape, first mitten like, and then with defined fingers. It flexed one hand, and then the other, its face shaping itself into a jelly-mould approximation of the Bursar's features.

The detail of the liquid man seemed to flush from head to foot. Here was an animated sculpture of the Bursar from the little hair combed over his head to the hand-made Italian boots, all done in a tasteful milky metallic acid, jelly-mould kind of a way.

The reincarnated Bursar zombie seemed satisfied with its appearance, and appeared to notice the three amigos for the first time.

Freddie and Hormoany already had their wands at the ready. Wandless, Parry was right behind them. Or more accurately, cowering behind them.

"So, we're talking 'Bursaratar II' here, are we?" Parry wondered aloud.

"*Anquishvay! Anquishvay!*" Freddie and Hormoany attacked together.

Little splatting noises were made as each spell hit, but the watery Bursaratar's surface seemed to sustain no more damage than thick custard, slapped by a teaspoon.

The Bursaratar swayed a little at the impacts.

"It's no good," warned Hormoany. "It's not working."

"We need more power!" cried Freddie. "Hold him off!"

He turned and grabbed Parry.

"Oi! What are you doing?"

"Needs must when the undead drive," said Freddie, turning Parry upside down and clasping him tightly by the ankles. Just as Hormoany had done a short while earlier, Freddie whipped aside the dressing on Parry's lacerated ankle, and, for good measure, added his own bite to those of the man-eating pansies.

Dropping Parry, Freddie turned back, pointing his wand at the walking acid bath. Hormoany was keeping up a rapid rate of fire, but the watery man was still managing to take slow steps forward, like a man against a gale. Half a dozen splash marks could be seen on its torso, yet the earlier spell damage had already healed over.

"*Anquishvay!*" shot Freddie.

A hole the size of a tennis ball was punched in the Bursaratar's shoulder. The avatar reeled and staggered backward.

"*Anquishvay! Anquishvay!*" Freddie blasted two more fist-sized holes in the moist menace, one in the side of the Bursaratar's head, one centrally into its chest.

"*Anquishvay!*" fired Freddie. Splat, went the spell, returning to teaspoon in custard efficiency.

"Damn!" swore Freddie. "I'm out!"

Hormoany turned and leapt upon Parry's ankle as he tried to crawl away.

"Ow!" cried Parry. "Get off!"

Freddie grabbed his other leg. "Sorry, Parry. It's the only way."

"If I'd wanted to be bled to death," complained Parry, "I would have just handed myself over to my parents."

"Right?" asked Freddie.

"Right," agreed Hormoany.

They turned just as the last of the damage Freddie had inflicted on the acidic zombie repaired itself.

"*Anquishvay!*" they both fired together.

A melon-sized hole burst in the liquid Bursaratar's chest. Its arms wheeled as it tried to hold its balance and then fell, splashing backwards.

"Is it dead?" asked Parry.

Freddie took half a step forward. He could see the liquid already reshaping the damaged chest. "I don't think so. In fact, I'd go as far as to say *RUN*!"

The Bursaratar drew itself back up to its feet, looking down at its own chest as the liquid flowed back into shape. As it finished you could never tell that the avatar had ever been injured at all.

The zombie saw the dust kicked up from the dry earth, showing it which way the teenagers had fled. It took one step forward, and stopped instinctively. Looking down, it saw a puddle of its own acid spilled by the force of the last wand blast. It pointed his toes at the liquid. The acid flowed into the watery body, making it complete once more. With that slow but purposeful walk the Bursaratar II set off in pursuit of Parry, Freddie and Hormoany.

The outbuildings behind the school were a maze. Duelling rooms, practice rooms, pavilions, print works, heating systems, storerooms and long-forgotten classrooms through which the trio weaved their way.

As Hormoany rounded a corner first, she stopped so suddenly that the two boys bumped into her. There, ahead of them, was the Bursar.

Not in liquid form, nor with the blank expression of the undead. Just as large as life, and very nearly as opaque, but you could just make out some of the shapes behind him if you really tried. And, if you looked carefully, he was making the rookie

and the seamy side of magic

ghost mistake of walking just above the ground. But it was definitely the Bursar.

"Go away!" cried Hormoany and, pushing her way past the boys, led them in the opposite direction, away from the Bursar's ghost.

Suddenly, there was the ghost again, in front of them.

"Wait!" he called. "I'm here to help you! This way," he said, pointing left.

"Yeah, that's likely," said Freddie.

They pelted off right, but suddenly, there again was the Bursar's ghost. "Look, I've come to help you fight, fight that *thing*."

"And just why are you changing sides all of a sudden?" challenged Freddie.

"Don't you know? Freddie, your brothers are *here*," the Bursar said, trying to indicate the spirit world by waving his hands to the heavens. "Something about a contract for stopping me, or it. Whatever."

"And you're helping because…?" enquired Parry.

"Because I don't want to spend the rest of eternity locked in the chalkboard in Artorius Smudge's room. That man's lectures are more boring than mine, and I was deliberately slowing time, just to make you lot suffer longer!"

"Fair enough," said Freddie. "What do we do, then?"

"He's coming!" screamed Hormoany, as the liquid Bursaratar II turned the corner.

"Quickly!" advised the ghost Bursar. "Get to the kitchens."

"Look," said Parry, "if you want to help us fight it, you go ahead and fight it."

"What, are you mad?" demanded the ghost. "I've only been dead five minutes. If you think I've had time for a pottery class and lessons in poltergeist technique at the local rail station, you're sorely mistaken. Now run! I'll see what I can do."

The zombie sloshed forward. The ghost Bursar squared up to him. "If I had some blotting paper," he said to his silvery reflection, "you'd be in real trouble."

The liquid Bursaratar regarded the spectral image for a few moments, then decided on a right hook. The punch swung completely through the ghost.

"Now," said the ghost Bursar, "I think it's my turn." He turned up the cuff on his right hand, pulled back his fist, and summoning every ounce of concentration, punched his fist through the liquid Bursar's head.

It didn't even cause a ripple.

The Bursaratar tried to grab the ghost, his arms flailing, going straight through the ghost as if it was not there. As indeed, in many respects, it wasn't. The ghost tried to jab and hook and uppercut, but all to no avail.

At roughly the same time they both seemed to reach the conclusion that neither one could hurt the other.

"Well, really!" said the ghost. "How very ridiculous." He popped out of this particular existence.

୨୦୧

The three of them fled to the main building. The Bursar's ghost was there, waving them inside.

"Why the kitchens?" called Hormoany.

"Do we need really sharp knives?" asked Parry.

"Or," panted Freddie, "are we going to distract him with a really good slap-up dinner?"

The ghost Bursar was again ahead of them when they reached the bottom of the stairs. The kitchens were huge, running all the way under the Great Hall and back still further, divided by long, solid preparation benches dotted with hobs, ovens and storage cupboards, above them hanging more pots and pans than anyone could conceivably require in a lifetime of avoiding washing-up.

"Quiet here, isn't it?" Hormoany commented on the suspiciously deserted kitchen. Raw food lay upon preparation tables, pots boiled and frying pans burnt their contents, as if all abandoned hurriedly.

"I'll admit," said the Bursar's ghost, "it was busier when I first looked in…"

But Parry was looking for a weapon. He grabbed a meat cleaver from a wooden chopping board.

"No!" hissed the ghost. "No, that sort of weapon won't harm it. It's just made of liquid. Now, extremes of temperature. That could do the trick."

There was a splatting sound on the stairs. A slow and steady progress was being made by the animated acid bath.

"The ice cabinet!" cried Hormoany, yanking open the heavy metal door. "Give us a hand!"

Snatching an ice pick each, Hormoany and Parry broke up the heavy blocks of ice as Freddie hefted them out, smashing them onto the floor. Three big blocks, and the Bursaratar II came into sight.

The three teenagers backed off instinctively.

Trudge, trudge, trudge, went the liquid Bursar as it waded through the ice. It began to slow and stiffen as its lower limbs turned into an icy sludge.

Trudge.... trudge.... trudge.

For a moment the liquid Bursaratar couldn't pull its foot from the floor, and then with an icy crunching sound its leg sheared apart below the knee. Standing like a man with one foot in a hole, it looked down at its broken appendage, and then at its other frozen leg. Even as the Bursaratar solidified it tried to cry out, but that, too, was frozen on its lips.

Freddie took aim with his wand.

Hormoany pushed the tip down. "Freddie! What are you going to say?"

Freddie paused for a moment. "I was going to say 'guano happens'."

"No. Let me do it. Mine's much cooler." She raised her wand and pointed it at the frozen figure of the Bursaratar II. "Arrivederci, sucker," she said, then, "*Anquishvay!*"

The frozen Bursaratar exploded into a thousand tiny pieces.

"Way to go!" exclaimed Parry.

But even as he said the words he realized the mistake. Already, in the heat of the kitchen, the ice was melting. As the fragments of frozen Bursaratar melted they started clumping together. "Once more, may I suggest – *RUN*!"

The three were off again, as the liquid Bursaratar pulled itself together. Hormoany was first to reach the far door – and bounced off the threshold.

"It's a binding spell! It's locked us in!"

"I didn't think avatars could cast spells, ghosts neither," puzzled Freddie.

They turned, peering through the hanging pots and pans and the steam of the bubbling cauldrons.

They could see the silvery glint of the Bursaratar as it began its slow and methodical march up and down between the worktables. Hormoany scrambled over to the nearest counter for cover, followed by the boys.

"The ghost said, 'extremes of temperature'. The ice just slowed him down," hissed Hormoany. "We're going to have to get him to the cauldrons."

"You notice, of course, that the ghost didn't actually stick around," commented Parry.

Hormoany nodded towards the top wall where maybe two-dozen huge cauldrons simmered away, each in its own fireplace. She peered over the worktop, and caught a glimpse of the Bursaratar turning the corner of the preparation benches, down at the bottom end of the kitchen.

At least his search pattern meant that he would have to walk up and down the great kitchens a dozen times before he reached them.

"Right," said Hormoany, pulling one of the Weasel brothers' charges from her from her pocket, struggling with the tight fit. "Freddie, we must swap wands for a minute."

"Ri-ight," said Freddie uncertainly.

"Parry. You're going to have to draw his attention up to the top end of the kitchen. We need to get him close to those cauldrons. Freddie, when he gets to the top I need you to blast him to slow him down for a moment. Then I'm going to stick him with this charge and detonate it with your wand."

"Hey!" said Freddie. "How come you're going to blow up *my* wand?"

and the seamy side of magic

"Look," said Hormoany, "we've got no time to argue, and anyway, my wand was a present from my sister. You don't think I'm going to blow *that* up, do you?"

"Parry," she said, slipping a knife from the worktop, "Freddie's going to need a drop more of your blood if he's to make sure of stunning the thing."

"Hey," objected Parry, "I think I've been bled enough for one lifetime. Freddie will just have to do his best without my blood."

"Well, fair enough, I suppose," said Hormoany.

"Ow!" cried Parry.

"Sorry, but it *is* important. Now you're bleeding anyway, just let Freddie have a drop."

Freddie grabbed Parry's wounded arm. It wasn't like Parry was going to have a choice in the matter.

"Now, Parry, it's important that you keep his attention up at the top end of the kitchen. It'll give me a chance to sneak round behind him. Freddie, get as close as you can and blast him with the wand from close range. I'll stick him with the charge, and detonate it. I'm the fastest on my feet."

"Yeah," wondered Parry. "How the hell do you do that?"

"Well, isn't it obvious? My shoe enchantment spell is obviously better than yours."

"What enchantment spell?" the two boys said together.

"Oh, honestly! Don't tell me you've been running around all day under your own power! You're hopeless! No wonder you've been panting like Mr Gardner in the showers."

"He doesn't pant in the showers," said Freddie.

"He does when us girls are in there. Now, places."

Parry peered over the top of the preparation bench. "Not that I'm complaining, but why is he taking so long?"

"No idea," replied Freddie, "but don't knock it."

The Bursar had a fastidious nature, both in this world and the next. Currently the liquid zombie was tidying the preparation stations as it went along, wiping a knife here, straightening a spoon there. Returning spices and condiments to their racks, and placing dirty dishes in the regularly spaced sinks. The food burning on the hobs seemed to be of no concern, only the orderly arrangements of the pans in which it charred.

"Oi, damp patch!" cried Parry. "I've seen wet weekends scarier than you!"

The Bursaratar's watery eyes turned towards his quarry. Parry was by the cauldrons, waving his arms. "Oi, you washout, come and get me if you think you're hard enough," he taunted.

The Bursaratar turned to face him. Obviously of the opinion that it *was* hard enough, the avatar finished folding a dishcloth and hung it on a door handle, then proceeded with its slow, purposeful walk.

Squelch, squelch, squelch, squelch.

"Come on! You're not fit to keep goldfish in!" cried Parry, trying to hold his nerve.

"NOW!" shouted Parry, diving between the preparation benches.

"Oi, waterworks!" yelled Freddie, popping up from behind a bench. He levelled Hormoany's wand: "*Anquishvay!*"

The Bursaratar turned towards Freddie, just in time for its face to explode under the wand blast. It staggered. Half its head was splashed out into a ragged cone shape.

"Now, Hormoany!" Hormoany dashed out from behind the Bursaratar and plunged the deadly lolly stick combination of wand and charge into the Bursaratar's back.

Its exploded face was already drawing itself back together, but still with only the one damaged eye the Bursaratar couldn't quite focus on the thing floating in its stomach. It made an ineffectual grab for it.

"Hasta la vista, sweetie," said Hormoany, relishing the moment; "*Etonated!*"

The Bursaratar realized what it was just in time for its torso to be rent in two by the force of the blast. One half of the torso rolled to the left, the other, with its nearly reformed head at right angles, swayed fifteen degrees or so from the vertical. An inhuman wailing came from the watery mouth:-

"*I need a sabbatical!*"

"Good," thought Hormoany, "but not good enough."

and the seamy side of magic

She grabbed a huge steel skillet and slammed it into the swaying creature with all her not-inconsiderable force.

The Bursaratar, unbalanced, staggered backward, hitting the rim of a boiling cauldron just below waist height. Its head and left half of the torso tipped over into the water, followed by its legs and the remaining right-side torso. Bubbles burst violently from the hissing cooking pot.

A face, frozen in a scream, appeared momentarily on the surface. An arm waved uselessly, and then the soup returned to its simmering. Freddie and Parry peered at the cauldron.

"Do you think it's…?"

Hormoany took a slurp from a long-handled ladle. "Urgh. Needs salt."

"We've kept our part of the bargain," whispered a familiar voice in Parry's right ear.

"Indeed we have, Damian," whispered a voice in Parry's left.

"We'll let you know when we need the blood."

"We've left a Will, with instructions, in Jude's room."

"By the time you get back the blood should be dry."

"And where there's a Will…"

"…there's a way."

The voices faded.

"Doesn't anyone," asked Parry plaintively, "know how to stay dead around here?"

There was a slow handclap from behind them. Parry, Hormoany and Freddie turned.

"Well done, I must say. It's rare that anyone gets the better of one of my re-creations." A tall wizard in black robes approached them, heels making a slight metallic clicking noise on the floor. "Of course, if you want to get a job done…"

"And you would be…?" asked Parry.

"Of course, where are my manners," said the wizard. "I am He-Who-Cannot-Be-Pronounced, but you may call me…"

Hormoany, Freddie and Parry stared at him expectantly.

"Brian," he said, holding out one hand, fingers splayed.

"Well, hi Brian." Parry half-heartedly returned the apparent wave. "But we've had a very busy day, and we'd just like to be going. Er, ah! Tell me," said Parry, addressing his friends, "is anyone else…?"

"Stuck?" ventured Freddie.

"Yes, that's the word."

"Yep," said Freddie.

Hormoany added, "Me too."

"I would love to chat, to get to know one another," said Brian-Who-Cannot-Be-Pronounced, producing a drinking straw which tapered to a needle-like point. "I'd love to discuss my plans for world domination, and my wicked revenge upon Bol d'Areth and his accursed apprentice, but I really haven't the time."

He grabbed Parry by the hair and snapped his head backwards.

Raising the straw to stab Parry's throat, he glimpsed something around his son's neck. "Oh, my dear boy," said He-Who-Cannot-Be-Pronounced, "what do we have here?"

He put his hand under the chain and lifted it out, until he could see the amulet. "I wonder what this is?"

A bolt of red lightning tore from the stone of Jape's amulet and ripped into He-Who-Cannot-Be-Pronounced, lifting him bodily from the floor and slamming him down, maybe a dozen paces further away.

The power holding Parry, Freddie and Hormoany was suddenly released. The three of them fell to the floor.

He-Who-Cannot-Be-Pronounced lay spread-eagled, his arms and legs splayed stiffly out.

"Ask – a – stupid – question." Brian forced his eyes to look at one of his hands, and wriggled the fingers. Then, with obvious effort, he started to flex his elbow.

"So we meet again, O unpronounceable one." Jape stood at the other end of the kitchen. "Oh, how the mighty are fallen!" He wandered leisurely towards He-Who-Cannot-Be-Pronounced. "I see you found my amulet, then."

"And you are?" He-Who-Cannot-Be-Pronounced managed to roll onto one side to see his adversary. "Ah, Mephisto!"

"Oh, it's first name terms, is it, Brian?" asked Jape. "Interesting sword of yours, this," he commented, twirling the

and the seamy side of magic 211

weapon in his hand. "The Bursar was kind enough to leave it to me, in his death throes, of course."

"Hey," said Freddie, "we killed him too."

"Twice," added Hormoany.

"Much as I'd like to talk over old times," said Jape, as He-Who-Cannot-Be-Pronounced managed to rise to his knees, "I do have to do something I should have done years ago."

He swung the sword down towards the throat of He-Who-Cannot-Be-Pronounced, but with an unexpectedly fast reaction He-Who-Cannot-Be-Pronounced raised one hand, his fingers spread wide. The blade struck the air in front of the hand as if it were solid, coming to a jarring stop.

"Don't you know," said He-Who-Cannot-Be-Pronounced, rocking back on his heels and standing full height, "it's not polite to behead anyone with their own enchanted sword." He raised his wand as Jape pulled the sword from the invisible barrier.

"So, after all this time," said Jape, "we'll finally see who is the better wizard."

"We know," said He-Who-Cannot-Be-Pronounced, "who the better wizard is, but this time I shall end it permanently."

"Come on!" hissed Freddie, crawling to a side wall. "We need to get out of here."

"I haven't got the strength to stand," said Hormoany.

"Me neither," said Parry.

"*Come on.*" With Parry and Hormoany following on all fours, Freddie reached the first hatchway. He opened it, and hundreds of black beetles tumbled out, many scurried away, this way and that. Grabbing a handful to stuff in his mouth, Freddie moved to the next hatchway. Unbolting the hatch he opened it first just a crack, and then wide. "Come on. This one's empty."

"Where are we going?" asked Parry, as he crawled into the stone tunnel behind the hatchway.

"These tunnels are used for storage," said Freddie. "They're filled from up top. With any luck, it's our way out."

"How do you know?" asked Hormoany.

"Oh, my brothers and me used to play 'Hide the Body' in these tunnels. Oh," he said, a thought clearly occurring to him. "Try and avoid the loose stones."

Locked by powerful magics, Jape's sword and the wand of He-Who-Cannot-Be-Pronounced swung this way and that; the sword slicing through metal, wood and stone like a hot knife through butter; the wand blasting anything it was pointed at into the next world, and probably a little into the world after that.

"Oh, this is such fun!" cried He-Who-Cannot-Be-Pronounced. "We should have done this years ago!"

ೞೞ

The darkness was lit only by Hormoany's wand. "I thought you said you knew where you were going."

Freddie peered around the chamber. "It's this way," he said, indicating one of the tunnels.

"No," said Hormoany. "That's the way we came in."

"Is it? Oh, must be this one then."

ೞೞ

Knives threw themselves at He-Who-Cannot-Be-Pronounced. Raising his hand, he froze them in mid-air. "Nice try, Mephisto, but you know I've always been better at this sort of thing."

A boiling cauldron tipped itself over, its contents rushing towards Jape's feet.

ೞೞ

Freddie thumped on the hatchway. "No, definitely locked."

"Damn," said Parry. "Do we have to go back and find another way?"

"What about a wand blast?" asked Freddie.

"Are you mad?" Hormoany replied. "It would probably bounce around in here and kill all of us. Anyway, I've got a better idea. If I can turn sand into stone…" she tapped where the metal frame was anchored into the wall, "...I should be able to turn the stone into sand."

ஒ

Jape fell backward as the sword was wrenched by unseen power from his hand. It flew to He-Who-Cannot-Be-Pronounced. He gave it an admiring look for a moment, and spun the blade. "Much better."

Jape shuffled backwards, scrambling on his hands and heels, and pulled himself up on the edge of a bench, flourishing his own wand at his nemesis.

"Oh," said He-Who-Cannot-Be-Pronounced, "we *do* want to make a fight of it to the last. Very well. Have you ever danced with the devil by the light of the silvery moon?"

Jape stared at He-Who-Cannot-Be-Pronounced, a little perplexed.

"Oh, I'm sorry, I'm just trying that out as a little thing to say before dispatching my victims. At once mysterious, romantic and threatening, a lot like me. What do you think?"

ஒ

"Do you have to make quite so much dust?" coughed Parry.

"Some people," sniffed Hormoany. "There, I think that should do it. Freddie, put your shoulder into it."

ஒ

Magical forces crackled between the two wands. Jape backed slowly away, his eyes frantically searching the room for anything he might use to his advantage. A silo hatch burst off the wall, and came crashing from a man's height to the floor. Parry, Freddie and Hormoany came tumbling down after it.

He-Who-Cannot-Be-Pronounced took advantage of Jape's distraction. The enchanted sword came slicing down through Jape's wand. The magical energy released, the wand exploded in Jape's hand. He fell on one knee, clutching his injured arm, acrid smoke rising from his seared fingers.

"Now this," gloated He-Who-Cannot-Be-Pronounced, "is a moment to remember."

"Strike me down now," warned Jape, "I'll become more powerful than you could ever imagine."

"Hm. Let's see..." said He-Who-Cannot-Be-Pronounced. Keeping the sword pointing at Jape's throat, he reached with his wand hand to pull out the amulet he was wearing around his neck. "I don't think so. I saw your trick with the Bursar. Very good, I must say. But this, you see, is an anti-morphic field charm. So I'm afraid this is not *au revoir*, my dear friend. This," He-Who-Cannot-Be-Pronounced swung the sword in a wide arc, "is goodbye."

Jape's severed head hit the floor.

It looked irritated.

"Good to see you back," He-Who-Cannot-Be-Pronounced addressed the three friends. "It's always pleasant to have one's triumphs witnessed."

"Great escape plan," hissed Parry. "We're all of four paces from where we started."

"The *theory* was fine," protested Freddie.

"It's no good, you know," said He-Who-Cannot-Be-Pronounced. "I reinforced the spells around these kitchens. You really can't get out. Now, where did I drop that straw?" He looked around the devastated room. "Up here, wasn't it?"

"You know," said Gordon, "I really wouldn't bother. I don't believe you'll be needing it."

෴

Bol d'Areth checked his new golfing hat in the mirror. He selected his sturdy number one wood from his golf bag, raised it onto his right shoulder and swung it across to the other.

He glanced out of one window and saw the wisps of smoke coming from the kitchen chimneys. Then he looked out across the fields in the other direction, and made for his office door.

∽∼

"So," asked Gordon, "how have you been keeping, dear brother?"

"Brother?" mouthed Hormoany, incredulously. "So that means, you're Gordon's nephew Parry!"

"That makes me feel a lot better."

"Well," said Freddie, "goes a long way to explain your limp handshake."

"Ha, ha, ha," said Parry mirthlessly.

"How is our dear father?" asked Gordon.

"Oh, you know – still dead," said He-Who-Cannot-Be-Pronounced.

"And your mother?"

"I'll get round to killing her in time. How's *your* harlot of a mother, Gordon?"

"Now, now," said Gordon. "Just because our father was something of a scoundrel, there's no need to blame mumsy."

"I am the legitimate seventh son, Gordon," said He-Who-Cannot-Be-Pronounced. "You know if you stand in my way I will destroy you."

"Now isn't that funny?" said Gordon. "There I was thinking I was the seventh son."

"You are a…"

"Now, let's not use the 'B' word. It's so ugly and unnecessary."

"You are illegitimate. *I* have the power."

"Oh really," said Gordon. "If you think *that* makes a difference."

He-Who-Cannot-Be-Pronounced raised sword and wand. "Have you ever danced with the devil by the light of the silvery moon?"

"Just the once," replied Gordon, flourishing a thin silver wand. "Lord of the Dance he wasn't, I assure you."

∽∼

Bol d'Areth stood on the school playing field, his eyes searching the boundary between the manicured lawns and the unkempt forest. Recognizing the right spot, he set off at a determined pace.

※

The enchanted sword exploded into a thousand fragments. His sword arm useless, He-Who-Cannot-Be-Pronounced defended himself with the wand in his other hand.

"Parry, I need your blood!"

"Bog off!"

"But Parry," cried He-Who-Cannot-Be-Pronounced, "*I am your father!* We could rule this realm and the mortal world together, side by side."

"But don't you need to drain him of all his blood?" asked Hormoany.

"Well, yes," conceded He-Who-Cannot-Be-Pronounced.

"So you mean," said Freddie, "that he can help you rule from the inside."

"You know, I'm very good with avatars," called He-Who-Cannot-Be-Pronounced. "*Abracadaver* has always been something of a specialty of mine."

"If it's all the same to you," said Parry, "I'd rather just watch Gordon whip your butt."

"You know, it didn't have to be this way," said Gordon, his wand discharging one powerful blast after another at his weakened foe. "But it was always one more dark art to master with you, one more minion to control. You just couldn't be content, could you, Brian?"

"What?" cried He-Who-Cannot-Be-Pronounced. "You want me to fade away, discussing my vegetable patch and this year's flowers?"

"There are worse things, you know."

"I could never be content living in the shadow of another."

"Bol d'Areth?" asked Gordon. "Oh, you know, he's not that bad as long as he gets four square meals a day. He's a pussycat, really."

"Well, I'd love to stay and chat," said He-Who-Cannot-Be-Pronounced, "but you know, I think we'll have to do this another time. Raising two avatars and beheading one old foe really is about my limit for the day."

"Oh, shame," said Gordon. "And I was so enjoying the family reunion."

He let off a vicious set of blasts at his half-brother, who spun, covering his head with his cape.

The cape fell to the floor, empty.

"You've killed him!" yelled Hormoany, delighted.

"I fear," said Gordon, picking up He-Who-Cannot-Be-Pronounced's cape, "I've had no such luck. What ghastly material."

"He escaped?" asked Parry.

"Translocated," explained Gordon. "A talent he and I share. About the only thing I did inherit from our father."

"So he's got away," stated Parry. "Free to come back for my blood another day."

"No," said Gordon. "I don't think so."

✼

He-Who-Cannot-Be-Pronounced materialized. He was standing on grass, looking at the forest's edge. He glanced over his shoulder. There, in the distance, was the school building.

"I'll be…" he began.

The last thing he saw was the business end of a golf club swinging at head height.

Bol d'Areth leant over the prone body.

"Fore!" the Headmaster called, belatedly.

✼

Bol d'Areth entered the school by the main doors, just as Gordon and his young friends reached the top of the service stairs from the kitchens. "Everything satisfactory, sir?" asked Gordon.

Bol d'Areth gave an affirmative grunt. "New tree bordering the forest," he said. "Crab apple."

"I see," said Gordon knowingly. "I'll tend to it."

"I don't understand," said Parry.

"Is He-Who-Cannot-Be-Pronounced…" began Hormoany.

"Going to be well looked after?" finished Gordon for her. "Yes. And not a word to anyone."

EPILOGUES

They kissed passionately, their young and eager hands hungry for one another's touch in these precious snatched moments of privacy.

Marie fell backwards onto the bed, her boyfriend Jason glued to her mouth. They threw the thin cover over themselves even as they wriggled out of their few remaining items of clothing.

"Oh," panted Marie, "oh, darling, are you sure you should be here? Wont they miss you at the – *oh yes* – the Kwadwaq club dinner? I mean, you are – *hmm nice* – you are the Captain."

"Errr hmm? Shhh, don't worry my love. Gribson will cover for me. Lets just...*oh Zeus*..."

"But isn't this – *oh there* – isn't this the time for honesty my sweet."

"Erm?"

"I know your secret," Marie reached toward the bedside table, slipping the loosely draped cover away from the crystal ball she had concealed. Within the ball was the image of another Jason, clearly finding something very funny amongst a rowdy crowd of his mates. "I don't mind, honestly."

Jason stared into Marie's eyes for a few moments. Then his shape blurred, shifted, and resolved into Goodie Deux-Pantoufles.

"You really don't mind?" Goodie asked.

"Well, girls who live in glass houses..." Marie waved her hand toward the crystal ball. The image zoomed out a little until another Marie could be seen, laughing as hard as the other Jason had been.

It was about then Goodie spotted the roving eye and a shell, a roving ear, hovering alongside the bed.

"I do hope your father won't hear of this," Marie's shape shifted and blurred. "Of course, your brother Martin would never forgive me, either," said Gordon.

Goodie's screams would have been enough to wake the dead, had Damian and Hannibal not been enjoying the set-up as much as everyone else in the Sade common room.

Dr Wendell of Ebbsfleet Community Comprehensive School stared at the thick foliage that blocked his way into his office. He pulled the small bottle from his pocket. It looked like a Persian perfume bottle, but the attached label said 'Magi-Gro'.

He opened the tag, and once again read the note inside.

'From Gordon, with compliments.'

Then he turned the tag over.

'Warning,' it read. 'Dilute one to one hundred thousand before use.'

"Mr Bailey, Mr Winston," he said urgently to the teachers flanking him, "get down to the tool shed, get gloves, saws, axes, Bowie knives – whatever – and get yourselves over to Miss Henderson's."

"Sir?"

"I gave her a drop of this stuff for her house plants yesterday. And the poor woman grows cacti, the saints preserve her."

And under the bridge, the troll waited.

THE END